CONFIDENTIAL

SUPREME HEADQUARTERS ALLIED
EXPEDITIONARY FORCE
EVALUATION AND DISSEMINATION SECTION
G-2 (COUNTER INTELLIGENCE SUB-DIVISION)

THE
NSKK OF THE NSDAP

E.D.S./G/3

CONFIDENTIAL

SUPREME HEADQUARTERS ALLIED
EXPEDITIONARY FORCE
EVALUATION AND DISSEMINATION SECTION
G-2 (COUNTER INTELLIGENCE SUB-DIVISION)

THE
NSKK OF THE NSDAP

E.D.S./G/3

Published by

The Naval & Military Press Ltd
Unit 5 Riverside, Brambleside
Bellbrook Industrial Estate
Uckfield, East Sussex
TN22 1QQ England

Tel: +44 (0)1825 749494

www.naval-military-press.com
www.nmarchive.com

In reprinting in facsimile from the original, any imperfections are inevitably reproduced and the quality may fall short of modern type and cartographic standards.

CONFIDENTIAL

SUPREME HEADQUARTERS ALLIED EXPEDITIONARY FORCE
EVALUATION AND DISSEMINATION SECTION
G-2 (COUNTER INTELLIGENCE SUB-DIVISION)

B-A-S-I-C   H-A-N-D-B-O-O-K

THE NSKK

(Das Nationalsozialistische Kraftfahrkorps)

NATIONAL SOCIALIST

MOTOR CORPS

E.D.S./G/3
Compiled by MIRS (LONDON Branch)
From Material Available at
WASHINGTON and LONDON

TABLE OF CONTENTS

	Page
Foreword	1

PART I

DEVELOPMENT OF THE NSKK

1	Background	3
2	The Motorstürme der SA	3
3	The Original NSKK	4
4	The reorganisation in 1934	4

PART II

FUNCTIONS, ACTIVITIES AND SPECIAL UNITS

| 5 | | Scope of the NSKK | 6 |

Section A: Training

6	Motor Hitler Jugend	6
7	Wehrstaffeln	7
8	Training of Army Recruits.	8

Section B: Training for Civilian Needs

9	Driving Instruction.	8
10	Training of Women Drivers	8
11	Compulsory Refresher Courses	8
12	Specialist Courses	9

Section C: Police Functions

13	NSKK Verkehrsdienst (Traffic Control Service)	9
14	Issue of Licences	9
15	NSKK Streifendienst (Patrol Service)	10
16	Cargo Inspection Service	10
17	NSKK Verkehrshilfdienst	10
18	NSKK Wasser Polizei (River Police)	10

Section D: Service in Armed Combat Forces

19	Duty with Wehrmacht	11
20	NSKK Polizei	11
21	Rhein-Flotille, Donau-Flotille	11
22	NSKK Wehrmannschaftsstürme (Home Defence Companies)	11

Section E: Transport Services

23	NSKK Kommando Volksdeutsche Mittelstelle (HQ Command for the Resettlement of Repatriated Racial Germans)	12
24	Community Emergency Service	12
25	Transportstaffeln (Transport Battalions)	12
26	NSKK Verlegungskompagnie (Transfer Company)	12

PART II (continued)

Section F: Miscellaneous Units and Services

27	Salvage
28	Streetcars
29	NSKK Katastrophendienst (Emergency Service)
30	Tyre Collection
31	Collection Campaigns
32	Publications

PART III

ORDER OF BATTLE

Section A: Organisation and Strength

33	Structure
34	Motor Obergruppen
35	Motor Gruppen and Motor Brigaden
36	Standarten
37	Structure of Smaller Units
38	Motor Boat Units
39	Strength

Section B: Supreme Command of the NSKK

40	The Korpsführer and his Staff
41	The Munich Branch of the Staff
42	The Berlin Branch of the Staff

Section C: Schools, Training Centres and Sport

43	Schools in Germany
44	Schools outside Germany
45	National Authority for Motor Sport

PART IV

RANKS, UNIFORMS AND INSIGNIA

46	Ranks and Insignia
47	Headgear
48	Uniforms
49	Unit Distinctions
50	Special Insignia

PART V

THE NSKK TRANSPORTGRUPPE TODT

Section A: Development

51	Transport for the OT
52	Transport for SPEER Projects
53	Role in the Blitzkrieg
54	War in the Balkans

		PART V (continued)	Page
55		The Afrika Korps	25
56		The Eastern Front	25
57		The Channel Coast, and Other Theatres	25

Section B: Reorganisation from 1942 onwards

58	The Merging of Units	26
59	Transport Brigade SPEER	26
60	Transport Brigade TODT	27
61	Ersatzabteilung der NSKK (Replacement Battalion)	27
62	Legal Status and Discipline	28

Section C: Foreigners in the NSKK

63	Quislings and Conscripts	28
64	Escutcheons	29
65	Epaulettes and Badges	29
66	Command	30

Section D: Uniforms, Ranks, Emblems and Signs

67	Brigade TODT	30
68	Brigade SPEER	30
69	Ranks	30
70	Rank Insignia	31
71	Unit Emblems	32
72	Tactical Signs	32
73	Signs on Civilian Lorries	33

Section E: High Command of Transportgruppe TODT

74	The Eight Departments	33
75	Department Ia. Einsatz (Employment)	33
76	Department Ib. Quartiermeister (Quartermaster)	33
77	Department Ic. Nachrichtenwesen (Intelligence)	34
78	Department II Personal (Personnel)	34
79	Department III Gericht-und Rechtwesen (Legal)	34
80	Department IVa Amt Verwaltung und Wirtschaft (Administration and Economics)	34
81	Department IVb and Vk (Medical and Technical Sections)	35
82	Special Units under the High Command	35

ANNEXE A

ORDER OF BATTLE (PROVISIONAL) OF THE NSKK

Part One:	NSKK Motorobergruppen	A 1
Part Two:	NSKK Motorgruppen and Brigaden	A 3
Part Three:	NSKK Standarten	A 5
Part Four:	**NSKK Motorbootunits**	**A 40**

ANNEXE B

NSKK Gazetteer	B 1

Page

ANNEXE C

DIAGRAMS AND PLATES

ANNEXE D

ABBREVIATIONS

INDEX OF SUBJECTS

Supplement
   giving OB of Regts etc   After A 40

FOREWORD

The National Socialist Motor Corps is a Nazi Party formation which, in one phase or another of its many branches, may acquire the services of virtually any civilian motor vehicle in German-occupied territory and which directly controls car ownership and operation of vehicles in Germany proper. Wherever wheels roll for the German war effort, the NSKK will be encountered. It is definitely the most powerful and, so far as strength of personnel and number and types of motor cars are concerned, the largest motor transportation fleet in Europe today.

The NSKK is organised along three different structural lines. In Germany proper it maintains a regional command and unit organisation with well over 4,200 headquarters, lower echelon orderly rooms, schools and other establishments. In addition, this Party home organisation operates motorboat units which train Army and Navy personnel. The NSKK also participates in Wehrmacht and police operations.

The second organisational structure of the NSKK consists of a large number of technical and police branches and services organised in units along purely military lines. Its personnel functions in part as auxiliary police, especially on Germany's highway system.

The third unit within the NSKK is the NSKK Transport Gruppe TODT, which represents a motor transport formation operating directly under the ground forces of the Wehrmacht, the Luftwaffe or the Organisation TODT, Germany's outstanding construction and building formation.

The Transport Gruppe TODT thus is a field force, whose personnel have been committed to action. It may be accountable to the Waffen SS, although it is only a transportation service in the combat zone. The other two branches of the NSKK may be likened to the Allgemeine SS or SA formations of the Nazi Party.

Like the SA, the NSKK enjoys a monopoly in the pre- and post-military training of the Wehrmacht man-power supply where drivers for motor transport, armoured reconnaissance and tanks are concerned. Like the NSFK, the NSKK supervises the technical training programme for a branch of the Hitler Jugend (Hitler Youth Organisation), namely the Motor HJ.

The peace-time strength of the NSKK is estimated to have been about 700,000. Active members in 1940 numbered more than 500,000, but by 1942 the membership had fallen to 220,000. However, to these figures should be added more than 100,000 Motor HJ boys training under NSKK control. The field forces of the NSKK -- all the services and component units of the Transport Gruppe TODT -- may total well over 200,000 men, which figure partly explains the decrease in the home formation.

From a politico-military point of view the NSKK should not be under-estimated either in terms of Allied field operations or in relation to the occupation of Germany. The National Socialist Motor Corps is definitely to be counted as one of the fully indoctrinated defence and security organisations on the German home front.

It presents a substantial counter-intelligence problem as a potential source of disaffection during and after the initial stages of Allied occupation. At the same time, the NSKK as an organisational network may be a ready instrument in the hands of Allied regional commanders, at least during the period immediately following victory.

While the personnel and organisational structure of such a Nazi formation must be neutralised, it is likely that Allied Authorities controlling the NSKK upon Allied entry into Germany will also control every motor vehicle in the Reich, other than those of the Wehrmacht.

PART I

DEVELOPMENT OF THE NSKK

1. **Background**

The variegated history of the NSKK (National Sozialistisches Kraftfahr Korps -- National Socialist Motor Corps) reflects the history of the Nazi movement itself. Like the Party, the NSKK has its roots in two different, almost diametrically opposed social classes; members of these two groups were employed in conducting, as it were, a political double pincers movement in the Party's rise to power, its "Battle for Germany."

One group was the mass of men uprooted by the war -- the youths who, because of the inflation, felt themselves condemned to permanent unemployment; the small shopkeepers who were threatened by the competition of the rapidly developing chain stores; all the unsettled veterans of the first World War who insisted that "something had to happen" to fill the emptiness in their lives. For these men the Party was a "Socialist" movement, and red was the primary colour of the swastika flag. This group was represented in the special units of the SA (Sturm Abteilung -- Storm Troopers), such as the Motorstürme der SA (Motorised Companies of the Storm Troopers).

The other group was that part of the German upper class which, fearing to lose old privileges in a social turmoil, hoped for a "strong hand" to keep down the growing waves of lower class dissatisfaction. To them the Nazi Party appeared to be only one of the many nationalistic movements of post-war Germany; the Party flag for them showed the old black, white and red colours of the imperial Second Reich.
They were organised into the motorised units of both the SS (Schutz Staffel -- Protective Detachments) and the NSKK and represented an aristocracy of "car owners."

Both of these forces were put into the limelight according to political requirements, employed to offset each other and to prevent the strengthening and stabilisation of the Weimar Republic.

2. **The Motorstürme der SA**
The Motorstürme der SA, or SA-Motorstürme, were organised on a country-wide scale on 15 May 1931, the organisation following closely the usual SA pattern.
Several Motorstürme (Motorised Companies) formed one Motorstaffel (Motorised Battalion).
The Gruppenstaffelführer (Commander of Motorised Units of an SA Group Command) was under the direct command of the SA Gruppenführer (Commander of an SA Group Command).
The position of the SA motorised units was similar to that now held by the cavalry units of the SA (SA Reiterstandarten).

In 1933 each SA Brigade made the attempt to organise a Motorstaffel or a Motorstandarte (Motorised Regiment), the latter comprising from two to five Staffeln.
Both the present insignia and identifying colours of the NSKK Motorgruppen (Group Commands) and the numbering system still conform in part to a pattern reminiscent of their former subordination in the SA.

The Nazi Party allotted to the SA motorised units the task of raiding buildings and entire street blocks inhabited by elements hostile to the HITLER movement; or undertaking "punitive expeditions" into areas and factories which were strongholds of the various "Marxist" parties, and of spreading terror and disorder -- the essential prerequisites for the growth of a Fascist movement.

3. The Original NSKK

The NSKK proper was founded on 1 April 1930, with HITLER as No. 1 member. Its first Korpsführer (Commander-in-Chief) was Captain PFEFFER von SALOMON, who, at the same time, held the post of Supreme Commander of the SA.
When Adolf HÜHNLEIN took over the NSKK command, at the end of 1930, the Corps totalled only 300 members. By the end of 1931 its active membership had risen to 10,000.

The NSKK appealed primarily to the wealthy factions in Germany which favoured the Nazi Party at the time of its struggle for power but were not desirous of engaging themselves in the political activities of the rank and file of the Nazi movement. To meet the special demands of these groups and to enlist their support, an NS Automobil Klub was founded, which, however, never developed, partly as a result of the reluctance of the upper classes to join.
Although the NSKK never did consist solely of car owners, its outstanding function was to place privately owned cars and lorries at the disposal of the Nazi Party and, in particular, of its shock formation, the SA. Thus the Party could efficiently transport its militant followers to its meetings held in neighbouring cities, and was able to concentrate its formations at parades and pageants which, on occasions, outnumbered the local anti-Nazi population.
The Party was in a position to carry its propaganda to the remotest hamlet of the Reich. "Without the automobile, without the loudspeaker, without the airplane we could not have conquered Germany," HITLER explained.

Typical of old-time NSKK members are such men as NSKK Gruppenführer Eugen HADAMOVSKY, present Chief of Staff of the Party Propaganda Office; NSKK Brigadeführer Dr. Roland FREISLER, President of the People's Court; NSKK Obergruppenführer Richard PRINZ von HESSEN, Commander of the Motorgruppe HESSEN, and August PRINZ zu HOHENLOHE, NSKK Standartenführer z.b.V. (NSKK Colonel, for special assignment on the NSKK General Staff).

As the SA Motorstürme of the '30s played a role during civil strife not unlike that of shock troops in wartime, the NSKK functioned as the motorised troop transport formation. Both organisations contributed decisively to the tactical mobility of the Nazi Party and thus to its successes.

4. The Reorganisation in 1934

After the RÖHM blood purge and the following relegation to a lesser status of the SA, the Motor-SA was taken out of the structure of the SA and united with the original NSKK; the two became the "sole motor organisation of the Nazi Party" (Order of 23 August 1934). The membership of this enlarged combined organisation increased soon to 350,000. After undergoing a new reorganisation in 1938, it reached a total membership of 500,000 in that year.

Adolf HÜHNLEIN continued as head of the new NSKK formation until his death on 18 June 1942. HÜHNLEIN was a former major of the Imperial German Army, a member of the EPP Free Corps and, for a time, general staff officer in EPP's 7th Reichswehr Division at Munich. Members of the Reichswehr company which he commanded protected HITLER's first meetings. Like HITLER, he served a fortress sentence at LANDSBERG, in Bavaria.

HÜHNLEIN had become Quartermaster of the NSDAP in 1925, and was subsequently named Korpsführer of the NSKK after von SALOMON's removal. He had also been appointed as Honorary Leader of the Motor HJ (Hitler Jugend), the motorised branch of the Hitler Youth Organisation. He attained the rank of Major General in the Regular Army, and in 1939 was appointed by GÖRING as Beauftragter für den Motorisierten Transport der Kriegswirtschaft (Trustee for Motorised Transport in War Industry), with the special mission to prevent waste of fuel and loading space.

Finally, he was installed as head of the Oberste Nationale Sportbehörde für die Kraftfahrt (ONS -- Supreme National Authority for the German Motor Sport). After his death the name "HÜHNLEIN" was conferred on the former Motorgruppe "HOCHLAND", whose headquarters is at Munich, the "Capital of the Nazi Movement."

His successor, and the present Korpsführer, is NSKK Obergruppenführer Erwin KRAUS.

The merger of the Motor-SA and the original NSKK, described as "the organs of the political will to motorisation," was effected without difficulty, chiefly because both organisations had been employed interchangeably and many leaders held functions in the two units. HÜHNLEIN had early envisaged the future paramount task of the Nazi motor organisations: A contribution to the motorisation of the German Army.

The amalgamated organisation no longer reveals its heterogeneous origins.

PART II

FUNCTIONS, ACTIVITIES AND SPECIAL UNITS

5. Scope of the NSKK

The present activities of the NSKK cover a wide field -- "Wherever there are wheels, the NSKK is also represented." The NSKK has broadened its scope from those early days when it was used to break up meetings in villages or to drive a group of slogan-shouting SA men through neighbouring towns.

It began to train recruits for the Army, to patrol the highways, to haul wood and potatoes, to apprehend vagrants and, later, fugitive prisoners.

Its units were attached to the Army, the Luftwaffe, the OT (Organisation TODT) and the various police forces of Germany.

It now issues drivers' licences, and repairs and maintains cars in its own shops.

Its instructors teach the use of Producer Gas Motors, and the NSKK builds cars from salvaged material.

It is obvious that activities of such a wide range cannot be accomplished by a single organisational structure but demands a considerable variety of highly specialised units and component sub-units. The special service units of the NSKK, therefore, are described in the following sections together with their particular tasks.

A. MILITARY AND PARA-MILITARY TRAINING

6. Motor Hitler Jugend (Motorised Branch of the Hitler Youth)

In 1934, HÜHNLEIN and Baldur von SCHIRACH arranged for the "strengthening and guardianship", from a technical point of view, of the Motor Groups of the Hitler Youth by the NSKK. It was agreed that the Hitler Jugend should be responsible for the "necessary political and ideological" indoctrination while the NSKK was to take over driving and technical instruction. The boys are given a certain number of driving lessons and the more promising ones are sent to a six-week course at one of the Motorsportschulen (Motor Sport Schools) for more intensive training.

The purpose of these Sportschulen was frankly admitted by Obergruppenführer JÜRGENSEN: "Today we can confess without revealing any secrets, that these 'Sportschulen' did not have anything in common with 'sport' but the name. We did not teach the boys how to drive in a flower carnival parade. Today the soldiers of our Panzertruppen and of the transport units (Fahrtruppen) prove on the roads and across the grounds of Russia what they have been taught."

By the end of 1938, 187,000 youths had been trained within "the framework of the Motor Hitler Jugend." The graduate trainees received, in addition to a driver's licence, a Motor HJ Leistungsabzeichen (Motor Hitler Youth Proficiency Badge.)

The organisation follows the Hitler Jugend pattern as to units. It had a membership of over 100,000 at the end of 1938. Boys who undergo more specialised training in the NSKK are freed from the obligatory Labour Service.

Instruction includes every department of motor transport, mechanics, cross-country driving as well as repair work, maintenance and map-reading.

7. Wehrstaffeln (Motorised Home Guard)

A decree issued by HITLER on 27 January 1939 prescribes the pre- and post-military training of personnel for motorised units of the Wehrmacht; this activity must be considered a parallel to the basic training given in the SA Wehrmannschaften for general military purposes:-

"In the field of pre- and post-military training, I charge the NSKK in collaboration with the Army with the following duties:

All reserves for the motorised units of the Regular Army are to be trained during the year prior to their call-up by the NSKK.

Such training is to be undertaken in courses lasting several weeks in the Motorsportschulen of the NSKK and is to cover the use of Army vehicles.

All reservists (Soldaten des Beurlaubtenstandes) who are designated as drivers in the case of mobilisation will have driving practice within the set-up of the NSKK......

".......The NSKK can boast of having trained the drivers for 1, 876 companies of the Fahrtruppen (transport troops).

".......The Korpsführer, in co-operation with the Supreme Commander of the Army, will issue the detailed instructions."

As a result of this decree the following statement was issued by the NSKK:-

"By order of the Korpsführer and in agreement with the OKH (Oberkommando des Heeres — High Command of the Ground Forces), the NSKK will hold henceforth courses of two months' duration in motor instruction for the obtaining of the Kriegskraftfahrschein (Wartime Driving Proficiency Certificate), which is distinct from the regular pre-military training SA Wehrabzeichen (Defence Badge) awarded after completion of three months' military sports training.

"This Proficiency Certificate will be awarded to active NSKK men who have qualified for the driving licence, Class 4, and to eighteen-year-old members of the Hitler Jugend prior to their mustering who had (a) the Motor HJ Leistungsabzeichen or
       (b) driver's licence, Class 4, issued by the NSKK.

"However, the certificate will not be given to members of the Motor HJ in possession of a driving licence if their soldierly bearing, technical knowledge and proficiency are not of a sufficiently high standard.

"Whenever possible, persons in possession of the Kriegskraftfahrschein will, when called up, be drafted into the Panzertruppe and Fahrtruppe (mobile troops)."

The training in the Wehrstaffeln consists also of two courses: a three-month course of general pre-military training (the same as that held by the SA) and a two-month course of instruction in driving and practical training in work and repair shops.

8. **Training of Army Recruits**

By a special agreement between the NSKK and Col. Gen. GUDERIAN, at the time Inspekteur der Schnellen Truppen (Inspector of Mobile Forces) and now Chief of the German General Staff, the NSKK took over the training of prospective tank drivers in special eight-week courses.

Similarly, the motorboat units of the NSKK undertook the training of Sturmbootpioniere (Assault Boat Engineers) of the Wehrmacht, recruited mainly from the parallel Motor HJ units. Since the outbreak of the war, forty-five motorboats have been built on the Lake of Constance for pre-military training purposes, and NSKK and Army officers have taken instructors' courses there. A Schiffsführerschule (School for Boat Mates) of the Motorgruppe WIEN gives a six-month course in the handling of motorboats and other river craft.

It is obvious why, at a time when the Nazi Party was still not in power but the major opposition party to the German Government, the Reichswehrministerium supported the NSKK as of potential military value: in its ranks was to be found personnel which could be used easily in case of mobilisation mainly to supply motorised units with drivers for staff cars, with dispatch riders and repair personnel as well as with military instructors.

B. TRAINING FOR CIVILIAN NEEDS

9. **Driving Instruction**

According to an order of the Reich Minister of Transport, dated 6 November 1943, the NSKK is authorised exclusively to give driving instructions to civilians.

Persons who intend to apply for a driver's licence must address a request to the local "NSKK Fahrbereitschaftsleiter (an officer concerned with transportation and with liaison between the NSKK and the police) stating the reasons for the application. If the request is granted, the NSKK will give the necessary instruction.

All former private driving schools already have been taken over by the NSKK.

10. **Training of Women Drivers**

The shortage of man power and the huge demand for drivers by the Armed Forces has increased the need for women drivers, a concept formerly rather distasteful to the Nazis. The NSKK arranges special courses, fifty lessons of two hours each, in driving and in servicing of vehicles.

11. **Compulsory Refresher Courses**

The pressing shortage of skilled labour in the repair shops, as well as a shortage of spare parts, caused the Reich Minister of Transport to issue on 30 April 1944 a decree under which all drivers of buses, freight vehicles with a capacity of one ton or more, and tow vehicles, must attend a technical course in maintenance and repair of such vehicles conducted by the NSKK. The purpose of the order was to enable the drivers, although the training is often hasty, to handle lesser repairs themselves and to improve maintenance of vehicles.

Registration for this course is the responsibility of both the car owners and the drivers. The attendance will be credited on the driver's licence. After 1 January 1945 only drivers with such an entry will be permitted to operate their vehicles.

This decree not only gives some indication of the official position which the NSKK has attained but also exemplifies the organisational development and spreading of activities of this body. Its manifold tasks make it necessary to maintain a large number of branches throughout Germany.

12. Specialist Courses

The introduction of producer-gas driven motor vehicles has further increased the activity of the NSKK. Its courses are compulsory for all those who want to obtain an operator's licence. The NSKK Lehrsturm (Training Unit) "Bernd Rosemeyer," BERLIN, has specialised in the testing, operation and servicing of gas-generators. Fifteen thousand cargo vehicles driven by producer-gas were put on the roads between 1941 and the end of 1943.

The NSKK even arranged instructions in the servicing and handling of tractors and other modern agricultural machines for the Volksdeutsche "resettlers" from WOLHYNIA and BESSARABIA.

C. POLICE FUNCTIONS

13. NSKK Verkehrsdienst (Traffic Control Service)

The NSKK has assumed the function of an auxiliary police force because of both the increase in military traffic and the drain on the regular police personnel as more and more were called to the colours of the Waffen SS, Wehrmacht and SS Polizei. It appeared for the first time in public in this role when the bulk of the German Army was moved from the East to the West following the conclusion of the Polish campaign.

Identified units of this type include:
NSKK Verkehrsstandarte (Traffic Control Regiment), WIEN:
NSKK Verkehrsstaffeln (Battalions), BERLIN and HAMBURG;
a Verkehrskompagnie LEMBERG;
NSKK Polizeiverkehrskompagnie on the Eastern Front. A German document dated 21 Jul 43 identifies the following Verkehrs-

staffeln:-
VKS GROSS HAMBURG,
    Johnsallee 67 I
        HAMBURG 13
VKS BERLIN, Ch'bg
    Knesebeckstr 81
VKS WIEN, III,
    Metternichgasse 4

When the need arose, however, these units were sent bodily into front-line service. The NSKK Polizeiverkehrskompagnie, from VIENNA, for example, was committed to action in Russia.

These units also were engaged in Verkehrerziehungsdienst, and educational service to publicize and enforce traffic rules, especially in war-time conditions, by means of films, exhibitions and the posting of road warning signs.

14. Issue of Licences

The Reichsverkehrsblatt (Official Gazette on Traffic Regulations) dated 10 June 1944 states that in the future the

NSKK will be exclusively entrusted with the testing of applicants for and the issue of drivers' licences. Furthermore, the certificate for operation of producer-gas driven vehicles (BB-Schein or <u>Betriebsberechtigungsschein</u>) is issued only by the NSKK.

15. <u>NSKK Streifendienst</u> (Highway Patrol Service)

The NSKK, in conjunction with the Police, controls traffic on all highways. Its main duties are the checking of pleasure driving and the apprehension of fugitive prisoners of war and foreign workers, "vagrants" and Army deserters. This work is done under the control of the <u>Kriminalpolizeileitstellen</u> (Criminal Police Regional Command HQ's).

The members of this service have been accorded the same powers as are held by all regular police officials, and they are subject to police force discipline as well as to Party regulations. The <u>Motorstandarte</u> 33, for instance, was reported to have provided in one month 253 two-men patrols and carried out 8,268 traffic control operations.

16. Cargo Inspection Service

Drivers of commercial vehicles have to obtain a permit from the <u>NSKK Fahrbereitschaftsleiter</u> when making journeys beyond certain distances, fixed locally. (The shipment of goods from Vienna to Linz, for example, could better and more cheaply be accomplished by Danube water craft than by road transport, the authorities claimed.

The NSKK official ensures that all available space in the vehicles is utilised, and that the kind of transportation employed is necessary and efficient. Further, he will provide cargo for the return trip.

17. <u>NSKK Verkehrshilfsdienst</u> (Road Aid or Traffic Assistance Service)

White, square signs in blue frames are posted from 6 km. to 8 km. apart on highways. The centre of these signs shows a red dial, with the insignia of the NSKK above and a Red Cross below. The sign is illuminated and indicates the nearest telephone from which the <u>NSKK Zonenführer</u> (Road Zone Controller) may be called in case of accident. He will arrange for a doctor, for police assistance, for an ambulance, for a tow car and similar services, including even funeral vehicles. Doctors and midwives may ask him to provide transportation.

This service is mainly an accident reporting system, organised in road zones. The <u>Motorgruppe</u> HESSEN reported in 1942 that its units erected 525 call posts. (The area of this regional command at the time was divided into thirty-five zones. The <u>Motorgruppe</u> served thirty main roads and 2,650 km. of secondary roads.)

18. <u>NSKK Wasser Polizei</u> (River Police)

The <u>NSKK Motorbootstürme</u> (Motor Boat Companies) operating in the Danube, the Rhine, in Germany's main rivers, waterways and lakes are assigned as auxiliary waterways police to control all traffic and to maintain a permanent patrol service.

D. SERVICE IN ARMED COMBAT FORCES

19. Duty with Wehrmacht

In addition to the transportation service rendered by the NSKK, its units have occasionally been bodily committed to action, and incorporated into the branches of the Wehrmacht fighting forces.
It must be remembered, too, that the transportation units are armed and in the past have frequently seen action along lines of communication and in the rear areas.

20. NSKK Polizei (NSKK Police)

Former traffic auxiliary units were sent to the Eastern Front. During the campaign in Poland, NSKK detachments were employed in clearing forest areas of guerrillas and in serving as liaison units between German civilian occupation officials and the Army.
The NSKK Aufbaustab Krakau, or NSKK Organising HQ, (CO: Oberstaffelführer DIEDRICH) set up the NSKK Kurierkompagnie Krakau with personnel of the NSKK Motorgruppe OBERSCHLESIEN to serve as dispatch riders for the occupation authorities.
The NSKK Verbindungsstab TOULON (Liaison Staff) maintained a similar service in southern FRANCE.
NSKK Police and Traffic Companies have served on various fronts attached to SS-Police Regiments, but have not yet been identified.

21. Rhein-Flotille. Donau-Flotille (Rhine and Danube Fleets)

When the Dutch Army continued its resistance on the isles of the Rhine Estuary, the Wehrmacht called for and received assistance from the NSKK Motorbootstürme serving on the Rhine. These units took part in mopping up operations, later being incorporated into the German Navy as Rhein-Flotille. A similar flotilla, partly organised from NSKK motor boat units, has been formed to patrol the Danube.

22. NSKK Wehrmannschaftsstürme (Home Defence Companies)

These companies were formed in Lower Styria and Carniola. They are fully armed, and as field units are committed to action against Serbian and Slovene "terrorists and bands," side by side with the SA Wehrmannschafter of the Steirische Heimatbund, an SA affiliation.

E. TRANSPORT SERVICES

NOTE: All transport activities of the NSKK, except those services rendered by the NSKK Transportgruppe TODT — which are treated in a special chapter -- are listed in the following paragraphs.

23. **NSKK Kommando Volksdeutsche Mittelstelle** (HQ Command for the Resettlement of Repatriated Racial Germans)

The Soviet-German agreement covering the repatriation of Germans from the Baltic countries and Bessarabia involved a major transportation project, since arrangements had to be made for population exchange, shipment of goods, implements, any specially granted facilities, camps, transit stations, colonising tools and material for rebuilding homesteads.

The NSKK Kommando Volksdeutsche Mittelstelle, under the command of SS- and NSKK Obergruppenführer LORENZ, performed this task. The agency was said to have removed more than 200,000 Volksdeutsche ("racial Germans") from their original domiciles.

24. **Community Emergency Service**

As transportation became the crucial strain on the home front and as the railroads were more and more overburdened, NSKK units were charged with the hauling of food and fuel, and of sand bags for the Air Raid Prevention Service.

The Transport Flotte SPEER (M.T. Fleet SPEER -- CO: GF Willi NAGEL), consisting of more than a hundred cargo barges, shipped food and coal to Berlin. It also runs steamers for coastal traffic e.g. in Finland.

The Motorgruppe WIEN hauled lumber from the Vienna Woods to the Austrian capital.

NSKK Stürme were assigned also to auxiliary duties in assisting postal authorities, especially at Christmas time, and maintained a regular package delivery service.

25. **Transportstaffeln** (Transport Battalions)

These battalions were established to meet the different needs of the home front. However, they were also used to haul supplies even to the front and to railheads. An NSKK Transport Standarte "W" (Transport Regiment) has been reported and is believed to operate in conjunction with the Armed Forces (Wehrmacht).

The NSKK Motor Brigade HAMBURG has organised an NSKK Transport Staffel MOORWEIDE for the needs of the SA Pionier-Standarte EMSLAND (CO: Oberstaffelführer HELLMANCYK). See Basic Handbook, The SA of the Nazi Party, para 44.

26. **NSKK Verlegungskompagnie** (Transfer Company)

One such unit has been identified. Its task was to remove cranes and similar harbour equipment from the Channel coast when the invasion of England was cancelled and to transport it to Baltic seaports where it was needed for the supplying of the Eastern Front.

F. **MISCELLANEOUS UNITS AND SERVICES**

27. Salvage

The NSKK Bataillon DÖBERITZ, often referred to as "Das Technische Bataillon," mainly composed of auto mechanics, was at Dunkirk, attached to the Organisation TODT. It had the task of refitting abandoned British vehicles following the evacuation of the B.E.F. The unit was said to have put into working condition 4,500 of 6,500 abandoned cars and handed them over to the Regular Army. However, another German report concerning the same performance spoke of 1,000 vehicles which had been constructed from the parts of 5,000 found by the Germans at Dunkirk.

The unit later received the honorary name of "Bataillon DÜNKIRCHEN," and personnel wear an armlet with that inscription on the left lower arm. The unit's task continues to be the overhauling and salvaging and dismantling of captured enemy vehicles.

28. Streetcars

In 1944, the NSKK provided personnel for night service on the Vienna streetcar system, both drivers and conductors, "until enough women had been trained for that work."

29. NSKK Katastrophendienst (Emergency Service)

This service, operating under the command of the Reichsverteidungskommissäre (Reich Defence Commissioners), takes the form in some localities of NSKK Katastrophen Einsatz Staffel (Emergency Action Battalions) or NSKK Soforthilfe ("Immediate Rescue").

These units are charged with heavy rescue work, maintenance of ambulance service, removal of debris, clearance of bombed streets and roads, assistance in the execution of evacuation schemes and establishment of local emergency traffic systems in case public carriers break down. They are entitled to commandeer and requisition any available vehicle for such purposes.

Some of these units own motorcycles and maintain dispatch services for A.R.P. formations and the Feuer-Einsatz-Kommandos der SA (See Basic Handbook, The SA of the Nazi Party para 52).

A special school for officers of this service is established at SCHLOSS GRÜNBERG, in the SUDETENLAND.

30. Tyre Collection

As a result of an agreement with the Reichsstelle Asbest und Kautschuk (Rubber and Asbestos Control Authority), the NSKK is charged with the collection of tyres from all laid-up motor cars. These tyres are collected by the NSKK and sent to the Wirtschaftsamt (Economic Office) and Hauptwirtschaftsamt (Central Economic Office) which finally dispatches them to the Reichsreifenlager (National Tyre Depot). The Wirtschaftsamt notifies the car owners and the local NSKK unit collects the tyres.

A similar system is in operation for the collection of used oil.

31. Collection Campaigns

The NSKK plays an important part in all salvage and

collecting campaigns, e.g., the collection undertaken to provide the soldiers on the Eastern Front with blankets and with skis. The NSKK also has received considerable praise in Germany for its contribution to the <u>Winterhilfe</u> (Winter Relief) and its assistance in collecting for it.

32. <u>Publications</u>

The following periodicals are published officially by the NSKK:

<u>"Deutsche Kraftfahrt"</u>
<u>"Der NSKK-Mann"</u>
<u>"Kriegspost"</u>
<u>"ONS - Mitteilungen"</u>

PART III

ORDER OF BATTLE

A. ORGANISATION AND STRENGTH

33. Structure

The NSKK, like the SA and the SS, is a Gliederung (Formation), or component part, of the Nazi Party. The Korpsführer (Commander-in-Chief) of the NSKK is under the direct command of the Führer (HITLER). However, only one part of the organisational structure of the present NSKK is similar to the territorial structure of the SA and SS, namely the regular NSKK Standarten (Regiments). Most of the other units of the NSKK—e.g., the NSKK Verkehrsdienst (Traffic Control Service) and the NSKK Verkehrshilfsdienst (Road Aid Service)—are designed along functional lines.

Other NSKK units and services are established in accordance with the territorial districts which they serve. The Katastrophendienst (Emergency Service) covers the Reichsverteidigungsgau (Reich Defence District), for example.

The original territorial organisation of the NSKK divided Germany into Motor Obergruppen (Supreme Group Commands), Motor Gruppen (Group Commands), Motor Brigaden (Brigades), Motor Staffeln (Battalions) and Motor Stürme (Companies). There are, in addition, Motorboot Standarten (Motor Boat Regiments) and Motorboot Sturme (Motor Boat Companies).

34. Motor Obergruppen

The territory of the Reich is subdivided into eight [~~nine~~] Motor Obergruppen, which bear geographical names, such as, for example SÜDWEST or ALPENLAND. They vary widely in size, each Obergruppe consisting of two to five Motor Gruppen and/or Motor Brigaden.

While Motor Obergruppen normally control only Motor Gruppen and Motor Brigaden, there is one exception: the Motor Standarte (Regiment) 91 (SALZBURG) is not a component of a Gruppe or Brigade, but is directly controlled by a Motor Obergruppe, namely the Motor Obergruppe ALPENLAND. until Jun 44

Each Motor Obergruppe covers [~~generally~~] approximately two to five NSDAP Parteigaue (Party Districts), but its boundaries were [~~are~~] not identical with either those of the Party regions or of the SA.

As from 6 Jun 44, however, the policy of bringing NSKK (etc) territorial divisions into line with NSDAP gaue, came into force (see next para).

There are two Motor Gruppen—SUDETENLAND and NIEDERSACHSEN—whose assignment within a Motor Obergruppe is not known. The activities of the Motor Obergruppe NORD have been suspended for the duration of the war.

It appears that most of the Motor Obergruppen perform only limited operations, being rather administrative regional control inspectorates. Commanders of the Motor Obergruppen, who generally hold the rank of Obergruppenführer, make occasional inspection trips.

35. Motor Gruppen and Motor Brigaden

Twenty-nine [~~seven~~] Motor Gruppen and seven [~~four~~] Motor Brigaden represent the next lower territorial echelon in Greater Germany. The chief difference between Gruppen and Brigaden is that the latter are composed of fewer Standarten and generally cover a smaller area.

Although the Motor Gruppen and Motor Brigaden have developed from the former SA Gruppen (Storm Troop Command) regions, their boundaries did not, before Jun 44 conform with those of the SA. The NSKK Motor Gruppen and Motor Brigaden usually bear geographical names similar to those of the SA, and occasionally SA Gruppen and NSKK Motor Gruppen have the same name, although they covered different areas.

Each Motor Gruppe or Motor Brigade takes in one or two NSDAP Parteigaue, but its boundaries do not coincide with the Party districts. As from Jun 44, however, territories of NSKK motorgruppen & -brigaden (with exceptions) are to be made to coincide with and take the names of, party gaue. For details of development, s revised annex Introductory

Each Motor Gruppe or Motor Brigade is organised into three to seventeen Standarten, which, in turn, control NSKK operations over an area which may include several NSDAP Partei Kreise (Party sub-Districts).

36. Standarten

About 200 Motor Standarten are believed to be in existence; most of these have been identified. They are numbered by Arabic figures, and correspond closely to those of the SA Brigaden of which they were formerly organic components as SA Motor Staffeln. All original NSKK Standarten are numbered consecutively from 1 to 100.

Where the headquarters locations of the Motor Standarte and the SA Brigade are not identical, they are close by each other. For example: Motor Standarte 3 (ELBING) -- SA Brigade 3 (RASTENBURG); Motor Standarte 6 (DANZIG) -- SA Brigade 6 (DANZIG).

An exception to this rule is Motor Standarte 90 (KLAGENFURT) and SA Brigade 90 (WIEN).

When a new Motor Standarte is formed, it receives the number of a neighboring Standarte plus 100, 200, 300, etc., e., Motor Standarte 96 (KREMS), Motor Standarte 196 (LUNDENBURG), Motor Standarte 296 (ZNAIM), Motor Standarte 396 (BRÜNN); Motor Standarte 33 (DRESDEN), Motor Standarte 133 (EBERSBACH), Motor Standarte 233 (MEISSEN). Thus, the numerical designation of NSKK regiments above 100 are irregular and not consecutive.

The Motor Standarten of the Motor Gruppe SUDETEN, however, have been allotted numbers from 200 to 215, although the SA Brigaden of that region are numbered from 100 to 104.

37. Structure of Smaller Units

Each Motor Standarte is normally composed of up to six Staffeln (Battalions), the average being four. Staffeln bear Roman numerals from I to VI within each number Standarte. The numeral of the Staffel is written before the letter "M" for Motor while the Arabic numeral of the Standarte follows the "M". V M 56 thus means the fifth battalion of the Motor Standarte 56.

It is doubtful whether every Standarte has been sub-divided into Staffeln, since it seems likely that some weaker Standarten are directly organised into Stürme (Companies).

Each Staffel is composed of three to ten Motor Stürme (Motor Companies); the average is believed to be six. These Stürme bear Arabic numerals as follows: all Stürme of Motor Staffel I are numbered consecutively from 1 to 10; those of Motor Staffel II, from 11 to 20; those of Motor Staffel III, from 21 to 30, etc.

16.

This system permits local reorganisation of small echelons below regimental level.

The Sturm is divided into three to four Trupps (Platoons). Theoretically, the Trupp contains three to four Scharen (Sections of Squads). However, it seems that these units operate only on rare occasions such as foot parades and festivities.

38. Motor Boat Units

The NSKK has established motor boat units which are now serving as auxiliary police formations and as training units for Army and Navy recruits and prospective entrants, selected mostly from the Motor HJ. These units have been employed in testing new assault craft models for the Army Engineers and for the Navy.

Members of these units wear a uniform similar to that of the Marine SA. A dark blue steering wheel emblem, with the NSKK eagle superimposed, is worn on the left lower arm. One epaulette is worn on the right shoulder; for officers of the rank of Obertruppführer and upward this epaulette is dark blue and gold on a dark blue background.

Sturmführer and higher ranking officers wear gold-corded shoulder straps. Adjutant's aiguilettes, similar to those in the SA, also are worn. **All Motorboat units identified are given in Annexe A, part Four.**

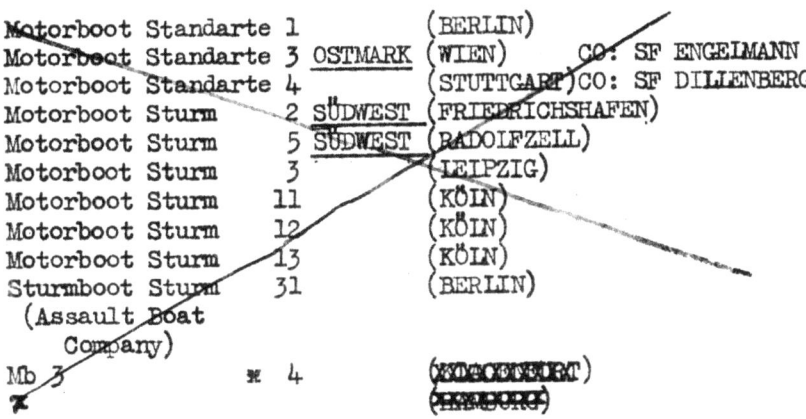

```
Motorboot Standarte   1             (BERLIN)
Motorboot Standarte   3  OSTMARK    (WIEN)           CO: SF ENGELMANN
Motorboot Standarte   4             (STUTTGART) CO: SF DILLENBERG
Motorboot Sturm       2  SÜDWEST    (FRIEDRICHSHAFEN)
Motorboot Sturm       5  SÜDWEST    (RADOLFZELL)
Motorboot Sturm       3             (LEIPZIG)
Motorboot Sturm      11             (KÖLN)
Motorboot Sturm      12             (KÖLN)
Motorboot Sturm      13             (KÖLN)
Sturmboot Sturm      31             (BERLIN)
 (Assault Boat
   Company)
Mb                    4
```

✱ The abbreviation "Mb" (for Motorboot Standarte) is used by the motor boat units in the same way the designation "M" is used by regular NSKK units.

39. Strength

The peace-time strength of an NSKK Standarte is 3,000 to 4,000 men. Since 200 such regiments are believed to exist, it is likely that the peace-time membership of the NSKK numbered about 700,000, a compromise total.

In 1940 the NSKK announced officially that its active membership had surpassed 500,000. By the end of 1942, however, its membership had decreased to 220,000. This drop was due to the extensive call-up following the initial failure of the campaign in Russia. To this figure must be added more than 100,000 members of the Motor Hitler Youth who, although not members and not under NSKK organisational control, operate under strict NSKK supervision.

An estimate of the strength of the NSKK Transport Gruppe TODT must needs be an approximation as its units and sub-units vary considerably as to strength and organisation. The NSKK Regiment NEDERLAND at one time was reported to total more than 10,000 officers and men, mostly Dutchmen. As other units of the Transport Gruppe TODT are likely to have a similar strength, the entire Transport Gruppe NSKK may well number more than 200,000 men.

B. SUPREME COMMAND OF THE NSKK

40. The Korpsführer and his Staff

The headquarters of the NSKK Supreme Command are divided, the administration of the formation being conducted from both Berlin and Munich: thus, Korpsführer KRAUS and his immediate staff have no definite headquarters.

KRAUS, NSKK Commander-in-Chief, ranks second to HITLER who, as head of the Nazi Pary, is Oberste Befehlshaber (Supreme Commander) of the Motor Corps.

An aviator during the first World War, KRAUS participated in the FREIKORPS activities of the post-war period in Upper Silesia and, later, in the Ruhr district. He joined the Nazi Party as early as 1923 and was active in both the original NSKK and the Motor SA.

From 1935 to 1942, when he was named Korpsführer after the death of HÜHNLEIN, KRAUS was Inspector of the Technical Training and Equipment of the NSKK. As HÜHNLEIN's successor, he is also Trustee for Motorised Transport in War Industry. He is a member of the Reichstag.

Stabsführer (Chief of Staff) of the Motor Corps is NSKK Obergruppenführer Ritter Adolf von DENK, a former Reichswehr officer and a careerist.

Following is a list of the chief administrative posts and the officials in charge, in the staff of the Korpsführer:-

Adjutant	(?) Adolf JÄGER
Leiter des Sonderstabes (Chief of the Special Staff)	GF E. J. NORD
Vorsitzender des NSKK Gerichtshofs (President of the NSKK Disciplinary Tribunal)	(?) Josef SEYDEL
Standartenführer z.b.V. (Colonel for Special Assignment)	SF August Prinz zu HOHENLOHE
Hauptamtschef (Chief Executive Officer)	(?) Prinz von HESSEN

41. The Munich Branch of the Staff

This branch is located at München, Briennerstr. 41. It contains the following offices, with the officials shown in charge:-

> Verwaltungshauptamt und Kassenwalter (Department of Administration and Treasury)
> Commanded by GF August KÖBELE

Organisationsamt (Department of Personnel and
 Administration)
Commanded by BF Theodor RULAND
Sanitätsamt (Medical Department)
Commanded by GF Dr. A. RIEDMAIER
Rechtsamt (Department for Legal Affairs)
Commanded by GF Ludwig TRENDEL
Inspektor für Technische Ausbildung und Geräte: München,
 Ständlerstr. 41 (Inspector of Technical Training and
 Equipment)
Inspektor für Ausbildung der Motor Hitler Jugend (Inspector
 of Training of the Motor Hitler Youth)
Stabskommandeur MÜNCHEN (HQ Commandant of Munich Branch)
Commanded by Ostaff Bruno NEY

42. The Berlin Branch of the Staff

This branch consists of the following:-

Abteilung Wehrsport (Department of Military Defence
 Training)
Musikinspizient (Inspector of Bands)
Ostaff EIX
Amt Presse (Department of Public Relations and Press
 Affairs)
GF Hans KREUZLIN
Amt Verkehr (Traffic Department)
Inspektor der Reichsmotorschulen: Berlin W 35, Graf Spee
 Str. 12 (Inspector of Automobile Schools)
Inspektor für Ausbildung: Berlin-Lichterfelde, Kyllmannstr.
 7 (Inspector of General Training)
Stabskommandeur Berlin (HQ Commandant of Berlin Branch)
BF Jost MARTIN

C. SCHOOLS, TRAINING CENTRES, AND SPORT

43. Schools in Germany

The NSKK maintains various types of schools both in Germany
and in occupied territories. These schools are under the control
of the Inspektor der Reichsmotorschulen. A list of those within
Germany follows:

The Reichsführerschule (National Officers' Academy of the
 NSKK) at
    Döberitz-Elsgrund
The Technische Führerschule (School for Officers of the
 Technical Services) at
    München, Ständlerstr. 41
Reichsmotorsportschulen (Motor Schools) at
    Aachen, Baden
    Bad Gandersheim/Harz (Gen. F.M. KEITEL Schule)
    Bayreuth-Saas
    Diez/Lahn
    Dramburg, Pommern
    Frankfurt/Oder
    Greiz, Thüringen

    Helsa bei Kassel
    Hülsen/Aller
    Itzehoe   (Adolf HÜHNLEIN Schule)
    Leipzig-Rochlitz
    Lyck, Ostpreussen
    Mittweida
    Mühlberg
    München-Gladbach-Rheindahlen
    Regensburg
    Schloss Grünberg, Sudetenland
    Schloss Hof, Sachsen
    Schweidnitz-Kroischwitz, Schlesien
    Schweina, Thüringen
    Schwerin
    Süchteln bei Krefeld
    Tübingen

Gebirgsmotorschulen (Schools for Driving in Alpine Terrain) at
    Hasslinghausen
    Holthausen bei Milspe (RUHRLAND)
    Kochel am See   (Gen. Ritter von EPP Schule)
    Kreiensen (Harz)
    Ottoweiler

<u>Schiffsführerschule</u> (School for Boat Mates) at
    Wien

44. Schools Outside Germany

The following schools have been identified, but the type of instruction is not known.

    Drammen, Norway
    Limburg, Belgium   ("NEDERLAND")
    Svelvir, Norway   (Drivers School)
    Zeesen, Holland

45. National Authority for Motor Sport

The <u>Oberste Nationale Sportbehörde für die deutsche Kraftfahrt</u> (Supreme National Authority for German Motor Sport) is a council headed by the NSKK Korpsführer. Its purpose is the official representation of the German Motor Sport at national and international racing competitions, the issue of international driving licences, the furtherance of motor sports, the examination of championship records, testing of new models, etc.

Although this agency, known as the <u>ONS</u>, is a governmental body, it is commonly considered to be a department of the NSKK High Command.

PART IV

RANKS, UNIFORMS AND INSIGNIA

46. Ranks and Insignia

The ranks of the NSKK and their insignia are almost identical with those of the <u>Allgemeine SS</u>. Officers and men below the grade of <u>Standartenführer</u> wear the rank insignia on the left collar patch. Standartenführer and higher officers wear rank insignia on both the right and left collar patches. The <u>NSKK Korpsführer</u> wears silver insignia, but all other insignia are aluminium. The piping of the collar patches for NCO's is black and aluminium entwined while that for officers is purely aluminium.

The NSKK ranks, their equivalent in the <u>Wehrmacht</u> and the corresponding insignia follow:

RANK	WEHRMACHT EQUIVALENT	INSIGNIA
Mannschaften (Other Ranks)		
Sturmmann	Grenadier	
Obersturmmann	Obergrenadier	2 stripes
Rottenführer	Gefreiter	4 stripes
Unterführer (NCO's)		
Scharführer	Unteroffizier	1 pip
Oberscharführer	Unterfeldwebel	1 pip, 2 stripes
Truppführer	Feldwebel	2 pips
Obertruppführer	Oberfeldwebel	2 pips, 2 stripes
Haupttruppführer	Stabsfeldwebel	2 pips, 4 stripes
Untere Führer (Junior Officers)		
Sturmführer	Leutnant	3 pips
Obersturmführer	Oberleutnant	3 pips, 2 stripes
Hauptsturmführer	Hauptmann	3 pips, 4 stripes
Staffelführer	Major	4 pips
Oberstaffelführer	Oberstleutnant	4 pips, 2 stripes
Höhere Führer (Senior Officers)		
Standartenführer	Oberst	1 oak leaf
Oberführer	Oberst (Senior)	2 oak leaves
Brigadeführer	Gen. Maj.	2 oak leaves, 1 pip
Gruppenführer	Gen. Lt.	3 oak leaves
Obergruppenführer	Gen. d. Inf.	3 oak leaves, 1 pip
Korpsführer	Gen. Feldmarschall	3 oak leaves within a wreath

In addition to the foregoing ranks the NSKK has a number of specialist grades such as <u>Schirrmeister</u> (Mechanic) and a <u>Verkehrsreferent</u> (Traffic Expert).

47. Headgear

NSKK men have three types of headgear: a crash-helmet of black fibre or leather, a field cap and a black forage cap. On the helmet the NSKK emblem is worn at the front; on the caps it is worn on the left side.

The visored service cap, shaped like a Norwegian ski cap, is made of olive-green material, has piping of dark brown and a black crown. Piping for officers of the grade of Sturmführer and higher is of aluminium. The staff of the Korpsführung (High Command), the staff of the Technische Führerschule and the staff of the Reichsführerschule wear caps with a carmine crown. The staff of the Motor Obergruppen have caps with a bright red crown.

In the front of the crown the NSKK wheel (a wheel with the NSKK emblem, a flying eagle with a wreath in its claws, the swastika inside the wreath) is worn.

Worn on the left side of the black forage cap is a triangular patch in the colour of the Motor Gruppe, with the NSKK emblem embroidered for all ranks up to that of Obertruppführer. Sturmführer and higher officers wear the emblem against a black background, with piping of twisted aluminium cord.

48. Uniforms

NSKK men wear the traditional brown shirt of the Nazi movement. The collar piping up to the rank of Obertruppführer is a black braid two millimetres wide. From Sturmführer upward, the piping is aluminium braid. NSKK men who are members of the Nazi Party wear the Party emblem on a brown necktie; non-Party members wear the NSKK emblem on the tie.

The tunic is made of olive-green material and has a dark brown collar. The trousers are black; they may be breeches worn with high black boots or regular long trousers as dress uniform. The overcoat has the same colour scheme as the tunic. NSKK men wear a long, grey raincoat.

NSKK personnel wear the NSKK emblems on the right upper sleeve, woven upon a green background on the overcoat and tunic and upon a brown background on the shirt.

The collar patch is always black, except for that of the HQ personnel of the Motor Obergruppen, the Korpsführung, the Inspectorates and the staffs of the Technische Führerschule, which is carmine, and that worn by the staffs of the Motor Gruppen OSTLAND, OBERSCHLESIEN and UNTERSCHLESIEN, which is bright red.

Rank insignia are worn on the left collar patch and the unit designation on the right.

The shoulder strap, worn on the right shoulder, is of black and white for all men up to the rank of Obertruppführer. The shoulder button is of silver. Motor Gruppen which have identical colours distinguish themselves by the figures 1 or 2 super-imposed on these buttons.

The base of the epaulette worn by HQ personnel is black, with a narrow carmine piping. Other personnel wear the piping of their Motor Gruppen. The colour scheme of the NSKK Motor Gruppen is generally identical with that of the SA Gruppen in whose territory they are located and with which their regional commands coincide most closely. This similarity in colour design resulted from a decree which was issued to "maintain the traditional liaison with the SA Gruppe from which these units originated."

49. Unit Distinctions

The following table sets forth the identified colours of cap pipings and emblem backgrounds used by the NSKK to distinguish units.

UNIT	COLOUR	BUTTON NUMERAL	ABBREVIATION
Korpsführung	reddish-brown		
Staffs of the Inspectorate	reddish-brown		
Staffs of Reich Schools	reddish-brown		
Staffs of Motor Obergruppen	reddish-brown		
Staff of M.Gruppe OSTLAND	bright red		
M.Gruppe WESTFALEN	maroon		Wf
OSTLAND	maroon	1	Ost
BERLIN	black		B
NIEDERRHEIN	black	1	Nrh
MARK BRANDENBURG	pink		Br
NORDSEE	dark green	1	No
THÜRINGEN	chartreuse		Th
OSTSEE	chartreuse	1	Os
WESTMARK	dark brown		Wm
NIEDERSACHSEN	dark brown	1	NS
SACHSEN	emerald green		Sa
NORDMARK	emerald green	1	Nm
LEIPZIG	emerald green	2	L
SÜDWEST	orange		Sw
FRANKEN	sulphur yellow	1	Fr
HÜHNLEIN	light blue		Ho +
SUDETEN	blue grey		Eg ++
HESSEN	navy blue		He

+   For HOCHLAND, the former name.
++ For EGERLAND, the former name.

Unit colour schemes and official abbreviations as used on documents, and collar patches for the other Motor Gruppen are not known.

50. Special Insignia

All members of the Motor Obergruppen ALPENLAND and of Motor Gruppen HÜHNLEIN wear an edelweiss of silver on the left side of their headgear.

NSKK men who have held membership in the Nazi Party SA, SS, HJ or the Stahlhelm prior to 31 Dec 1932 are entitled to wear on the right upper arm the Ehrenwinkel (Chevron) which distinguishes them as Alte Kämpfer (Old Fighters). For Austrians, the qualifying date for the chevron is 1 Jan 1937.

Ehrenführer (Honorary Leaders) wear on the left lower arm a black armlet with the inscription "Ehrenführer".

Führer z.b.V. wear on the left lower arm a black armlet with the letters "z.b.V." (Special Assignment).

The Tyr-rune, a symbol of loyalty in the form of an upward pointing black arrow, is worn on the left upper arm.

Men who have served for at least six months in the Verkehrserziehungsdienst (an educational service to enforce and publicise traffic rules) wear an NSKK emblem on a black escutcheon with the inscription "Verkehrserziehungsdienst". This is worn on the right upper arm.

NSKK men who speak a foreign language wear armlets indicating the language.

PART V

THE NSKK TRANSPORTGRUPPE TODT

A. DEVELOPMENT

51. **Transport for the O.T.**

In the Spring of 1938, the NSKK sent twenty dispatch riders to the Western frontier of Germany to participate as auxiliary message carriers in connection with the construction of the WEST WALL. Prior to that, NSKK units had assisted in the great road-building projects of Dr.Ing. Fritz TODT by establishing communications between the engineering headquarters and the construction sites.

The responsibilities of the NSKK in the building of the WEST WALL reached a point where the organisation was commissioned to transport all building material and workers to and from the fortifications. Special LKW Staffeln (Lorry Battalions) of the NSKK were established, eventually taking over the entire motor transport connected with the Organisation TODT (O.T.).

During the construction of the WEST WALL, according to one report, the NSKK carried 8,000,000 metric tons of building materials, its vehicles covering a total road distance of 60,000,000 km.

When the OT. was shifted to build the ATLANTIC WALL, the Staffeln of the NSKK went along, reorganised by that time into the Transport Standarte TODT.

52. **Transport for SPEER Projects**

In the years 1938-'39, large quantities of material had to be amassed in and near Berlin for the remodelling scheme of the city under the supervision of Ing. SPEER. In the autumn of 1939, GÖRING commissioned SPEER with the construction of new airdromes in the Reich.

Drivers were needed for these tasks, and SPEER called on the NSKK school at DÖBERITZ, near Berlin, for men to transport the material to the proposed sites. This work was done under the supervision of the NSKK Baustab SPEER (Construction Staff), and the drivers were organised in the NSKK Motor Transport Standarte SPEER (Motor Transport Regiment).

53. **Role in the Blitzkrieg**

During the campaign in Poland, NSKK units were first employed to provide the fighting forces with ammunition and fuel.

In the fighting in Norway, an NSKK Regiment appeared for the first time, equipped with Ford trucks, and supported the German Alpine troops in difficult terrain.

When the German offensive in the West began, the invading armies received rations and ammunition brought by NSKK formations, recruited from all parts of Germany, in addition to those furnished by the regular supply troops. The NSKK formations were responsible chiefly for the providing of supplies to rapidly advancing Panzer and motorized divisions and for maintaining an efficient courier service in sectors immediately behind the front. Most of these NSKK units were components of the Motor Transport Standarte SPEER, which soon was renamed the NSKK Motor Transport Brigade SPEER.

54. War in the Balkans

When the war spread to the Balkans the NSKK Einsatzgruppe SÜDOST (Front-Line Group Southeast) was formed. But the men of this group, even while carrying out their many varied tasks, soon had to fight against the partisans who attacked the motorized convoys. They had to secure the lines of communication. They directly supported the O.T. in the construction of roads on which the minerals of the Balkans were hauled to the industrial centres of the Reich.

55. The Afrika Korps

The Transport Brigade SPEER allotted its 4th Regiment to the Afrika Korps. In less than two years of operations, this regiment covered 4,700,000 km. and transported 290,000 tons of bombs, ammunition and fuel for ROMMEL's troops. This unit not only had to move supply dumps forward and backward, keeping up with the rapid advances and retreats of the armoured divisions, but also had to set up a considerable number of highly efficient mobile workshops and small repair stations attached to the lowest echelons along the lines of communications. The regiment shared the fate of the Afrika Korps, surrendering after bitter and stubborn resistance on 12 May 1943.

56. The Eastern Front

The biggest transportation task, however, was carried out in Russia. NSKK men had to maintain a constant flow of supplies in almost roadless territory under adverse weather conditions, contending meanwhile with unrelenting harassment by partisans. They had to operate as supply troops, repair units, police force and messenger service along the entire Russian front.

NSKK Kompanien and NSKK Regimenter were formed according to the initiative of front commanders and local needs.

During the period from November, 1942, to April, 1943, one NSKK regiment serving on the southern sector of the Eastern Front covered a total distance of more than 2,000,000 km. The columns of the regiment brought up approximately 210,000 metric tons of supplies during this period, a task which otherwise would have required the use of 660 railway trains of twenty-five cars each.

At Stalingrad, NSKK men fought in the line as mobile infantry.

57. The Channel Coast and other theatres.

Following the campaign in France, the principal mission of the NSKK in Western Europe became the transport of material for the Channel gun emplacements along the invasion coast, the supplying of bombs and the construction of airfields for the Luftwaffe's "Battle of England." Certain NSKK units, attached to and under the supervision of the Luftwaffe, were detailed to carry out the work on the last mentioned tasks.

In December, 1940, an NSKK Transport Brigade Luft, now referred to as the NSKK Motorgruppe Luftwaffe, had come into being. It had 6,000 personnel and 3,422 trucks. According to German press reports, this unit transported 65,000 metric tons of bombs in a single month.

The Transport Standarte TODT had by this time been reorganised into the Transport Brigade TODT, operating more than 5,500 lorries. This unit carried material for the construction of fortifications along the Atlantic coast.

A transport unit similar to that assigned to the Luftwaffe was established for the Army. The conscripted drivers were recruited principally from German home units of the NSKK. The unit was named the Transport Brigade HEER.

NSKK Regiments were also identified in Italy, Norway and Finland.

B. REORGANISATION FROM 1942 ONWARDS.

58. The Merging of Units

After the death of Dr.Ing. Fritz TODT, Professor Albert SPEER, the present Reich Minister for Armament and War Production, took over the Armament Ministry and the many other tasks assigned to TODT and inaugurated a reorganisation of the NSKK transport system. Korpsführer KRAUS and Minister Speer announced on 9 October 1942 that the existing units would be amalgamated and placed under command of NSKK Gruppenführer Willi NAGEL, who previously had been a Regierungsrat (Government Councillor) in the Polizeipräsidium in Berlin.

The present Transport Gruppe TODT comprises the NSKK Transport Brigade TODT, the NSKK Transport Brigade SPEER and the Legion SPEER. (The existence of the Legion SPEER at this time is no longer confirmed.)

The two brigades were organised along different lines in keeping with the demands which they had to meet. The following paragraphs deal with the components of the Transport Gruppe TODT.

59. Transport Brigade SPEER

The NSKK Transport Brigade SPEER is strictly a military unit, being organised into Regimenter, Abteilungen (Battalions) and Kompanien. The regiments and companies bear Arabic numerals, the latter numbered consecutively within each regiment. The Abteilungen are designated by Roman numerals, from I to V, within each regiment. It is not known whether the companies always form Abteilungen, but that is rather doubtful.

Ten regiments have been identified so far: two -- referred to together as the Transport Standarte HEER -- serve the Army; the other eight serve the Luftwaffe and are known as the Motorgruppe Luft. These units exclusively use their own organic vehicles.

The identified regiments are:-
```
    Transport Regiment  1    : In Russia
    Transport Regiment  2    : In France. Commander: Staffel-
                             : führer KIESSLING
    Transport Regiment  3    : In Italy.  Commander: Staffel-
                             : führer KOBLITZ, successor to
                             : Staffelführer KUNZ
    Transport Regiment  4    : Surrendered in Tunisia;  Com-
                             : mander: Staffelführer HAEFKE
 *  Transport Regiment  5
 *  Transport Regiment  6
    Transport Regiment  7    : In Northern Italy
 *  Transport Regiment  8
 *  Transport Regiment  9    :
    Transport Regiment 10    : In White Sea area
```

** NSKK REGIMENT NEDERLAND : In Russia, Commander: OGF
: BEYER-EHRENBERG

One battalion has been identified -- the Abteilung WIKING, which operated in the Lake ILMEN area of Russia.

---

* While these units have not yet been identified, their existence, at least for a time, appears to be certain, as the Transport Brigade SPEER is known definitely to have been composed of ten regiments.
** Numerical designation unknown.

60. Transport Brigade TODT

As the demand on transport varies widely in the O.T., the organisation of this brigade is decidedly elastic, without any prescribed formula for set-up or strength. Small and large units are frequently detached and employed for O.T. contractors and sub-contractors who have the most immediate need.

The highest HQ is the Abschnittsführung (Sector Command, about equivalent to a regimental echelon, although it may have a much greater personnel strength), as, for example, the Abschnitts-Führung SÜDOST.

The next lower echelon is the Kw. Transport Abteilung (Motor Transport Battalion), if the unit's own vehicles are to be used, or Transport Staffeln, if the vehicles are regularly leased or are requisitioned from civilian owners. These units are designated by Roman numerals, serially from I to V, for each Abschnittsführung.

The next lower units of the Abteilungen are the Kompanien. The Staffeln are made up of Hauptkolonnen (Main Columns). These subsidiary units in both cases are designated by consecutive Arabic numerals within the Abschnittsführung. The Hauptkolonnen are organised into ten Kolonnen (Columns) each. A Kolonne consists of twenty to thirty vehicles. The lower structure of the Kompanien is not definitely established.

Identified Abschnittsführungen of the Transport Brigade TODT are:

    Abschnittsführung WEST
    Abschnittsführung SÜDOST
    Abschnittsführung KAUKASIEN
Units known to be in existence include:
    Abschnittsführung NORWEGEN
    Abschnittsführung OST
    Abschnittsführung ITALIEN

61. Ersatzabteilung der NSKK (Replacement Battalion)

The replacement unit for the NSKK Transport Gruppe is the Ersatzabteilung der NSKK - Transport Brigade SPEER, in Berlin, Heerstrasse. Although it retains the original name of Brigade SPEER, it furnishes personnel to the entire Transport Gruppe, including the Transport Brigade TODT and the Legion SPEER. Most of the trained men are sent to the Transport Brigade SPEER. The training includes protection of convoys, removal of road barriers and demolition of abandoned motors.

The depot trains virtually all personnel for the Transport Brigade SPEER, but details principally NCO's for the Transport Brigade TODT. This is due to the fact that the SPEER units service the regular Armed Forces while the TODT men are only attached to the O.T.

62. **Legal Status and Discipline**

All members of the NSKK Transport Gruppe TODT, including the members of the Legion SPEER (non-Germans) are subject to the Militärstrafgesetzbuch (Military Penal Code). For this purpose the ranks of the Transport Gruppe had to be defined in relation to those of the Regular Army as follows:

Mannschaften:	Sturmmann
	Obersturmmann
	Rotenführer
Unteroffiziere ohne Portepee:	Scharführer
Unteroffiziere mit Portepee:	from Oberscharführer to Obertruppführer
Offiziere im Leutnants und Hauptmannrang:	from Sturmführer to Hauptsturmführer
Stabsoffiziere:	from Staffelführer upward

A Court Martial, however, may consider only the rank held in the Transport Gruppe TODT, while the rank held in the regular NSKK unit is subject to jurisdiction of and can be lost only by a sentence of a Parteigericht (Nazi Party Tribunal).

In this connection it is important to note that personnel in the Transport Gruppe TODT may have three unrelated different designations:
    (a) the rank held in the NSKK proper;
    (b) the rank held in the Transport Gruppe TODT and
    (c) the function exercised in the NSKK Transport Gruppe.

For example, a man may be a Sturmführer in the NSKK home organisation, a Hauptsturmführer in the Transport Gruppe TODT and a Staffel-Führer, i.e., a battalion CO.

In other words, in analogy to a member of the Allgemeine SS serving in the field force or Waffen SS, that man holds one rank in the Party formation, one in the unit serving on the front and finally fills a functional post.

The Transport Gruppe has also its own disciplinary tribunal, which may impose sentences up to six months' imprisonment. The President of this NSKK Gerichtshof is NSKK Staffelführer Dr. HEISE.

C. **FOREIGNERS IN THE NSKK**

63. **Quislings and Conscripts.**

As in the Waffen SS, the personnel of the NSKK have to a considerable degree been recruited from among Quisling pro-Nazis and forcibly conscripted men in occupied territories. A German newspaper once described it thus: "If you meet a young NSKK man, he is probably a Dutchman, a Frenchman or another foreigner; only the elderly men are Germans: they are the administrators and supervisors."

The first large contingent was recruited in 1941 from Dutch

volunteers and became the Regiment NEDERLAND. It now is a component of the Transport Brigade SPEER. A Motor Schule NEDERLAND, under command of OF. O. BURCKNER, was established in LIMBURG, Belgium.

In September, 1942, DORIOT's agents were offering 500 francs a month to North African natives who would serve as truck drivers for the NSKK.

As late as 24 June 1944, a notice appeared in the Netherlands newspapers, offering every Dutchman between the ages of seventeen and forty-five years the opportunity of entering as drivers into NSKK service. Those who had not yet learned to drive would receive preliminary training. According to the contract, the minimum period of service would be one year.

Those who are accepted are released from compulsory work in Germany. This last enticement is likely to have provided a strong stimulus for enlistment in the NSKK.

The Regiment NEDERLAND was sent to Russia, but large numbers of other Dutch volunteers saw service in Belgium and France. Some of these were forced to transfer to the Wehrmacht or Waffen SS and went into combat in the NSKK uniform.

Flemish and Walloon drivers were enlisted separately and most of them sent to France. French volunteers despatched to Russia and so-called Russian "Volunteers" formed the NSKK Einsatzgruppe RUSSLAND (Front-Line Group RUSSIA) of the Transport Abteilung V of Abschnittsführung WEST (in France).

Volksdeutsche ("racial German") NSKK men were put to use as Beifahrer (assistant drivers) to Croatian "volunteers" of the Abschnitt SÜDOST.

64. Escutcheons

Non-German NSKK personnel wear the same uniforms as do the Germans but may be recognised by an escutcheon on the left upper sleeve of the jacket and overcoat indicating their nationality.

A color plate showing escutcheons which have been identified appears in Annexe C.

65. Epaulettes and Badges

The piping of the epaulettes and the background of the NSKK badge worn on the field cap vary according to the national group to which the volunteer belongs. Examples include:

Walloons	Yellow
French	Blue
* AGRA	Rust
Dutch	Red
Flemish	Red and green

Non-German NSKK men wear a black forage cap with two small buttons in front and the regular NSKK badge, embroidered on a triangular background, on the left side. The badge is embroidered in black and silver thread, on the appropriate background.

---

* Amis du Grand Reich Allemand, a Walloon pro-Nazi "Cultural Society" which had formed a company composed only of the "elite" pro-Germans and race fanatics.

66. **Command**

The non-German companies are commanded by a German Hauptsturmführer (Captain), who is assisted by a Sturmführer of the same nationality as the personnel. It is believed that the rank of Sturmführer (Lieutenant) is the highest one which a non-German can attain.

Originally, all non-Germans serving in the NSKK were organised in the Legion SPEER. This unit operated only government-owned vehicles. Later, during the years 1942-'43, non-Germans were enlisted in all other units of the NSKK Transport Gruppe TODT (i.e., the two brigades -- SPEER and TODT).

D. UNIFORMS, RANKS, EMBLEMS AND SIGNS

67. **Brigade TODT**

Members of the NSKK Transport Brigade TODT wear normally an olive-green field blouse, black breeches, black belt and are generally armed with a side-arm or pistol. The black NSKK field cap is worn as headgear. In winter the olive-green NSKK greatcoat is worn, closed at the collar.

68. **Brigade SPEER**

Members of the NSKK Transport Brigade SPEER wear the grey-blue uniforms of the Luftwaffe, short boots and, usually, anklets.

Some units of the NSKK wear brown uniforms, not unlike those of the O.T., with a Gothic "Sp" on the right collar patch. Men thus uniformed were originally personnel of the NSKK Baustab SPEER, which is now incorporated in the NSKK Transport Gruppe TODT.

On the right collar patch of these uniforms is the regular NSKK badge, embroidered in black and silver thread. Rank designations are worn on the left collar patch. Senior officers above the rank of Standartenführer wear their rank insignia (oak leaves) on both collar patches.

69. **Ranks**

The ranks of the NSKK Transport Gruppe TODT are almost the same as those of the Waffen SS. Those of the regular NSKK resemble those of the Allgemeine SS.

Chief of the Transport Gruppe TODT is Gruppenführer NAGEL. His assistant is an Unterkorpsführer, who heads all the non-German NSKK units.

The other ranks and their parallel in the Waffen SS and the Wehrmacht follow:

NSKK	WAFFEN SS	WEHRMACHT

Höhere Führer (Senior Officers)

NSKK	WAFFEN SS	WEHRMACHT
Obergruppenführer	Obergruppenführer	General d. Inf.
Gruppenführer	Gruppenführer	Gen. Lt.
Brigadeführer	Brigadeführer	Gen. Maj.
Oberführer	Oberführer	Oberst (Senior)

Mittlere Führer (Intermediate Officers)

NSKK	WAFFEN SS	WEHRMACHT
Standartenführer	Standartenführer	Oberst
Oberstaffelführer	Obersturmbannführer	Oberst Lt.
*Staffelführer	Sturmbannführer	Major

Untere Führer (Junior Officers)

NSKK	WAFFEN SS	WEHRMACHT
Hauptsturmführer	Hauptsturmführer	Hauptmann
Obersturmführer	Obersturmführer	Ober Lt.
Sturmführer	Untersturmführer	Lt.

Unterführer (NCO's)

NSKK	WAFFEN SS	WEHRMACHT
Haupttruppführer	Stabscharführer	Hauptfeldwebel
Obertruppführer	Hauptscharführer	Oberfeldwebel
Truppführer	Oberscharführer	Feldwebel
Oberscharführer	Scharführer	Unterfeldwebel
Scharführer	Unterscharführer	Unteroffizier

Mannschaften (Other Ranks)

NSKK	WAFFEN SS	WEHRMACHT
Rottenführer	Rottenführer	Obergefreiter
Obersturmmann	Sturmmann	Gefreiter
Sturmmann	SS-Mann	Schütze

* The term Staffelführer is also used as a contraction of the functional designation "Führer einer Staffel" (Battalion CO.) and as such may also be written hyphenated, namely: Staffel-Führer. Thus signatures like the following may appear:-
    (a) NSKK Staffelführer Schmidt
                  Staffelführer (Battalion CO)
    (b) NSKK Sturmführer Schmidt
                  Staffelführer (Battalion CO)
    (c) NSKK Staffelführer Schmidt
                  Abschnitts-Führer (Regimental CO)

70. **Rank Insignia**

Shown on the left collar patch:-

Two thin stripes	Obersturmmann
Four thin stripes	Rottenführer
One pip	Scharführer
One pip, four stripes	Oberscharführer
Two pips	Truppführer
Two pips, two stripes	Obertruppführer
Two pips, four stripes	Haupttruppführer
Three pips	Sturmführer
Three pips, two stripes	Obersturmführer
Three pips, four stripes	Hauptsturmführer
Four pips	Staffelführer
Four pips, two stripes.	Oberstaffelführer

Shown on both collar patches:-

One oak leaf	Standartenführer
Two oak leaves	Oberführer
Two oak leaves, one pip	Brigadeführer
Three oak leaves	Gruppenführer
Three oak leaves, one pip	Obergruppenführer

Officers of the rank of Staffelführer and higher wear a thick silver-tressed cording on the epaulette.

71. **Unit Emblems**

A number of emblems for the Transport Gruppe TODT have been established. They are usually painted on the left front fender and on the left rear of vehicles.

Emblems appearing on vehicles consist of a square divided into two equal triangles by a diagonal line from the lower left to the upper right or vice versa, the left triangle containing the unit emblem. The right triangle contains two groups of figures separated by a horizontal line, the number of the Kompanie appearing above the line and the vehicle number appearing below. Above the square the letters NSKK are shown in Roman print.

Identified unit emblems include:

Transport Regiment 1	1 oak leaf
Transport Regiment 2	2 oak leaves
Transport Regiment 3	3 oak leaves
Transport Regiment 4	The outline of the Continent of Africa pierced by a spear (for SPEER).
Abschnittsführung WEST	A bunker cupola from which a gun barrel, pointing to the right, protudes.
Abschnittsführung SÜDOST	A turtle

In case emblems are used on arrows, road markers and signs, the letters NSKK precede the emblems, in other words, appear on their left. The emblem is in the centre, and the designation of the higher unit follows with the number of the Kompanie or Hauptkolonne appearing at the end behind a diagonal, as, for example, NSKK (emblem) III/9.

72. **Tactical Signs**

The following tactical symbols are in use to designate headquarters:

Regiments and Abschnittsführungen -- a square flag in a parallel square outline, with the flag showing the letters NSKK in the left upper corner, the unit emblem in the left lower corner and the word Stab (HQ) in the lower right corner.

For Abteilungen or Staffeln -- a triangular flag in a square outline. The flag may point either to the right or to the left and shows the letters NSKK along the top edge, the unit symbol in the lower corner and the number of the unit near the tip of the flag.

For Kompanien or Hauptkolonnen -- a rectangular flag in a parallel rectangular outline, the letters NSKK appearing in the left upper corner of the flag, the unit emblem on the lower edge in the centre and the unit number in the lower right corner.

73. **Signs on civilian lorries.**

Civilian-owned lorries requisitioned or commandeered by the NSKK Transport Brigade TODT have the following markings: On the right door a large white T flanked by small numbers for the Staffel and the Hauptkolonne, respectively, e.g., 1 T 2, the first, or left, number indicating the Staffel and the second, or right, number indicating the Hauptkolonne. On the left door of such vehicles a white NSKK eagle appears. On the left front fender a yellow ring centred by a white L indicates the Luftwaffe. It is believed that other letters indicate other attachments.

E. HIGH COMMAND OF TRANSPORTGRUPPE TODT

74. **The Eight Departments**

Gruppenführer Willi NAGEL, Führer (Commander-in-Chief) of the Transport Gruppe TODT, is assisted in the administration of that formation by:
The Adjutantur (Adjutant's Office) -- Staffelführer HEIDEL and Sturmführer GEITZ and:
The Haus-Revision (Financial Control Section).

Oberstaffelführer REUSNER, who ranks as Stabsführer (Chief of Staff), controls the eight Hauptabteilungen (Departments) of the Transport Gruppe TODT. These departments, which were reorganised in February, 1943, are set out in the following paragraphs. Numbering is that actually used in German.

75. **Department Ia Einsatz (Employment)**

Commanded by Ostaff. ILIG and organised into four Abteilungen (Sections):-

1. Planning und Aufstellung (Planning and Co-ordination).
    Commanded by Ostuf LANGHAMMER.
2. Einsatzüberwachung (Works Supervision)
    Commanded by Ostuf MANDT
3. Sondereinsätze (Special Activities)
    Commanded by Ostuf SCHOTTEN
4. Streifendienst (Police Patrol Service)
    Commanded by Ostuf GROSSER

76. **Department Ib Quartiermeister (Quartermaster)**

Commanded by Ostaff. REUSNER and organised into seven Abteilungen:-

1. Beschaffung OKH - Luftwaffe ("Procurement" High Command - Luftwaffe).
2. Zeugmeisterei (Equipment).
3. Waffenmeisterei und Heeresgerät (Ordnance and Material)
    Commanded by Kriegsrangführer HASSE.
4. Kfz. Lager und Ausrüstung (M.T. Depot, Stores and Shops)
    Commanded by Ostuf BLANCK.

5. Verbrauchsmittel (Fuel and Lubricants)
6. U.-Gerät (?)
7. Transporte (Shipments)

77. **Department Ic Nachrichtenwesen (Intelligence)**

    Commanded by Oberstleutnant (Wehrmacht) VOGEL and organised into three Abteilungen:

    1. Press, Archiv und Kriegsgeschichte (Press Relations, Archives and Historical Section)
    2. Abwehr (Counter-Intelligence and Espionage)
    3. Truppenbetreuung (Welfare of Field Forces)

78. **Department II Personal (Personnel)**

    Commanded by Ostaff REUSNER and organised into four Abteilungen, the first of which is divided into six sub-sections:-

    1. Personalverwaltung (Personnel Administration)
        Commanded by Ostuf GUTHARDT
        a. NSKK Angehörige und Wehrmacht, Führer (NSKK Members and Armed Forces, Officers)
        b. NSKK Angehörige und Wehrmacht, Mannschaften (NSKK members and Armed Forces, Other Ranks)
        c. Zivil (Civilians)
        d. Ausländer (Non-Germans)
        e. Statistik (Personnel Statistics)
        f. Mobstelle: (Mobilisation)
            Dienstverpflichtungen, (Recruiting, etc.)
            Sicherstellungen, (Bonds)
            Dienstzeitbescheinungen, (Service Certificates)
            Uk-Stellungen, etc. (Deferments)

    2. Gehalts-und Lohnwesen (Salaries and Wages)
        Commanded by Herr MARSCHALIK.
    3. Ausbildungswesen (Training)
        Commanded by Major (Wehrmacht) SPECHT.
    4. Ersatzabteilung (Replacement)
        Commanded by Ostaff GREULICH.

79. **Department III Gericht-und Rechtwesen (Juridical and Legal Matters)**

    Commanded by Staff Dr. HEISE and organised into:-

    1. Disziplinärgericht (Disciplinary Tribunal)
    2. Rechtshilfe und Klagesachen (Legal Aid)

80. **Department IVa Amt Verwaltung und Wirtschaft (Department of Administration and Economics)**

    Commanded by Verwaltungsführer SAMSE and organised into four sections, which, though styled Hauptabteilungen (Department), have, since the reorganisation of 1943, the status of Abteilungen (sections).

    Hauptabteilungen:-

    1. Verwaltung (Administration)

2. **Kfz.-Abrechnung** (M.T. Audit)

3. **Wirtschaft** (Economics)

4. **Bauten** (Buildings and Construction)

81. **Departments IVb and Vk.**

   The remaining two departments are:

   IVb Sanitätsabteilung (Medical Section)
   Commanded by **Stuf** Dr. SIKORSKI.

   VK Technik (Technical Matters)
   Commanded by **Staff** LAGRANGE

   Note: While all the foregoing eight offices are located at BERLIN 9, CHARLOTTENBURG, the office of an **Unterkorpsführer** has been reported in the West. He is believed to be in charge of all non-German NSKK men.
   OGF GRÜTKE has been mentioned as Commander of all NSKK units in northern France and Belgium.

82. **Special Units under the High Command.**

   The **Transport Gruppe TODT** maintains special units, which are administered directly by the High Command of the formation. They include:

   Sanitätskraftfahrzeug Staffel (Motorised Medical Battalion). Such a battalion has been attached to the Chief Surgeon of the O.T. proper. Its equipment includes mobile dental clinics, ambulances, lorries and automobiles. Its personnel strength is unknown.

   Winterdienst (Winter Service). Special snow removal equipment such as snow ploughs, etc., are owned by the O.T. proper, but are operated by personnel of the Transport Gruppe TODT. The repair shops used in this service and the personnel employed are both practically subordinated to the O.T.

   Streifendienst (Patrol Service). Each Regiment (SPEER) and each **Abschnittsführung** (TODT) have assigned a motorised patrol unit in order to control its personnel while on duty, to prevent desertion and to regulate traffic.

SUPREME HEADQUARTERS ALLIED EXPEDITIONARY FORCE
EVALUATION AND DISSEMINATION SECTION
G-2 (Counter Intelligence Sub-Division)

Introductory Note to the Order of Battle of the NSKK
(EDS Amendment of 8th February, 1945, to EDS/G/3)

REORGANISATION OF THE NSKK

The trend towards making German administrative regions correspond to Party Gaue is parallel to the trend towards equating the territories of Party Formations and Affiliated Organisations with Party Regions.

A reorganisation has therefore taken place within the NSKK as follows: in conjunction with the NSKK Korpsführer KRAUS, M. BORMANN, Chief of Staff of the Party Chancellery, ordered that as from the 6th June, 1944, the territories of the NSKK Motorgruppen and Motorbrigaden should be made to coincide with the boundaries of the NSDAP Gaue.

With the exception of the Motorgruppe "Adolf Hühnlein" (for traditional reasons) and the Motorgruppe "Niederrhein" (which at the present time covers three Gaue: Düsseldorf, Essen and Köln-Aachen) all the NSKK Motorgruppen and Motorbrigaden were to assume the names of the respective Gaue.

No doubt this reorganisation has now taken place, but as complete details have not yet come to hand, the following revised Order of Battle will show certain discrepancies. Thus our information to date shows 36 Motorgruppen and Motorbrigaden, as compared with a probable 40, (i.e. to correspond with the number of Gaue concerned), and in many cases the old names are still listed.

The reorganisation will also affect the Standarten in so far as the controlling Motorgruppe or Motorbrigade is concerned. The respective numbers and HQs of the Standarten will have remained the same, but in order to conform with the organisation according to Gaue, certain Standarten may now come under a different Motorgruppe or Motorbrigade.

NOTE: For supplementary information on the reorganisation of Party Formations, etc., see also Introductory Note in the Amendment of 29 Jan 45 to EDS/G/1 (on the SA).

ANNEXE A.

Order of Battle (Provisional) of the NSKK

NOTE: NSKK special units and services, including units assigned to the Wehrmacht, are not listed in this Order of Battle, but will be found in the text.
For all abbreviations, see Annexe D.

KEY:

PART ONE: NSKK MOTOROBERGRUPPEN (Superior Group Commands).

1. "COMMANDER": The last identified Commander is given, also his deputy (i.V., in Vertretung) where known.

2. "COMPONENT UNITS": Motorgruppen and Motor Brigaden have been listed as identified components. In the two cases marked with a question mark (?), the allotment is assumed, not definitely established.

PART TWO: NSKK MOTORGRUPPEN (Group Commands) and MOTORBRIGADEN.

3. "NAME": In brackets is given the former name, if any.

4. "COMMANDER": In addition to the commander, is given any staff officer identified.

5. "COMPONENT UNITS": Lists Standarten by their numerals. It should be specially noted that in many cases a Standarte has been assumed to belong to a certain Motorgruppe (or Brigade), either because of the series numbering (see text, para 36) or because of geographical location.
Where the two conflict, the series numbering has been taken as more conclusive.

PART THREE: NSKK STANDARTEN.

6. "NO.": Standarten numbers are complete up to 100. Beyond 100, the listing of any number, even without an identified HQ location, indicates that the Standarte is known to exist, while the omission of a number indicates that there is no evidence of the existence of such a Standarte.

7. "HQ LOCATION": As implied above, under Note 6, the entry "not identified" applies only to the HQ Location, not to the Standarte itself.

8. "COMPONENT UNITS": Lists the Motorstaffeln (Battalions) and Motorstürme (Companies) under the German system of numbering, i.e. Roman numerals for Staffeln, Arabic for Stürme, followed by the number of the Standarte (e.g. II M 10 = Staffel II of Standarte M 10).
This column has also been used in a few cases for the conferred honorary name of a Standarte.

PART FOUR: NSKK MOTORBOAT UNITS

9. Under the above heading have been grouped all available identifications of NSKK Motorboat Units; the grouping is based rather upon deductions than upon definite evidence.

ANNEXE A

Order of Battle (Revised) of the NSKK

NOTE: NSKK special units and services, including units assigned to the Wehrmacht, are not listed in this Order of Battle, but will be found in the text.

PART ONE

NSKK MOTOR-OBERGRUPPEN

NAME	HQ	COMMANDER	COMPONENT UNITS
ALPENLAND	Salzburg, Halleinerstr.	OGF MÜLLER-SEYFFERT	M.Brig. Kärnten M.Brig. Steiermark M.Brig. Tirol-Vorarlberg M.Brig. Salzburg
MITTE-WEST	Berlin W 62, Wichmannstr. 17	OGF SAUER	M.Gr. Franken M.Gr. Berlin M.Gr. Mark Brandenburg M.Gr. Leipzig ? M.Gr. Sachsen ? M.Gr. Niederrhein M.Gr. Hessen M.Gr. Thüringen M.Gr. Nordsee M.Gr. Westfalen-Nord M.Gr. Westfalen-Süd M.Gr. Magdeburg-Anhalt
NORD (temporarily not operating)	Hamburg, 21 Fährstr. 11	OGF Günther PRÖHL OGF JURGENSEN OGF THOMSEN, i.V.?	M.Gr. Niedersachsen M.Gr. Schleswig-Holstein M.Gr. Ostsee M.Brig. Hamburg M.Brig. Hansa
NORDOST	Danzig, Baumbachallee 7	OGF Otto SCHADE	M.Gr. Danzig-Westpreussen M.Gr. Ostland M.Gr. Wartheland
OST	Breslau, 1 Schweidnitzerstr. 6	OGF SCHEIBNER	M.Gr. Oberschlesien M.Gr. Neiderschlesien M.Gr. Sachsen ? M.Gr. Leipzig
SÜD	München, 23 Ohmstr. 15		M.Gr. Hühnlein M.Gr. Bayernwald
SÜDOST	Wien III, Metternichg. 4	OGF SEYDEL Stabsf. OF SCHELDES Adj. SF Hans MERTENS	M.Gr. Niederdonau M.Gr. Oberdonau M.Gr. Sudeten M.Gr. Wien
SÜDWEST	Stuttgart O, Neckarstr. 68	OGF WAGENER	M.Gr. Südwest M.Gr. Westmark M.Gr. Rhein-Mosel M.Brig. Schwaben

PART TWO

NSKK MOTORGRUPPEN AND BRIGADEN

NAME (Gruppe)	HQ	COMMANDER	COMPONENT UNITS
BAYERNWALD (Bayr. Ostmark) (Bayreuth)	Regensburg Lutherstr. 14	BF GUNTHER (OF RILLING ?)	77, 80, 81, 82, 181?
BERLIN	Berlin W 35, Graf Spee Str. 6	GF MEYER (GF JELEN ? i.V.)	25, 27, 28, 29, 30, 31, 32, Mb1 (?)
DANZIG-Wpr.	Danzig-Langfuhr Baumbachallee 7	OF Fritz WOLF	5, 6, 105, 106, 130
FRANKEN	Nürnberg W, Furtherstr. 19	OF HOHENBERG i.V. HORNDRASCH	78, 79, 83, 95, 187
HESSEN	Frankfurt a.M. Lindenstr. 7	BF Robert ALBER Stabsf. OF BARTE	46, 47, 48, 49, 50, 146, 147, 148
HÜHNLEIN (Hochland)	München 25, Plinganserstr. 72	OGF Emil SIMMERMANN	84, 85, 86, 87, 181?
LEIPZIG	Leipzig C 1, Otto Schillerstr. 3	OGF SCHNÜLL BF STEITZ (Stabsf.)	35, 36, 37, 38, 39, 137, 138, 141
MAGDEBURG-ANHALT	Dessau, Ruststr. 1	OF KÖSTER	135
MARK BRANDENBURG	Frankfurt a.O., Sophienstr. 5	BF JEHNE or OF HOFFMANN	22, 23, 24, 26, 112, 122
NIEDERDONAU	Wien III, Metternichg. 4	GF Erhardt HILLE	96, 97, 98, 196, 197, 296, 396
NIEDERRHEIN	Düsseldorf, Alte Garde Ufer 3	OGF Hans KLUG Stabsf. SF SCHNEEWIND	71, 72, 73, 74, 75, 76, Mb "RHEIN" (?)
NIEDERSACHSEN	Hannover O, Hindenburgstr. 37	GF Arnold KLENKE	51, 58, 59, 60, 61
NIEDERSCHLESIEN	Breslau 1, Schlossplats 4	OF STRECKFUSS Stabsf. KÖSTER	18, 19, 21, 118, 120
SCHLESWIG-HOLSTEIN	Kiel, Knooperweg 57	BF Theodor SCHMIDT	14, 15, 16, 115
NORDSEE	Bremen, Delbrückstr. 18	OF LEHMANN OF LUEBKE i.V.	62, 63, 160
OBERDONAU	Linz, Postlingbergstr. 30	GF DÖRFLER	99, 100, 199, 299
OBERSCHLESIEN	Kattowitz, Ludendorffstr. 23	BF W. LUSCHERT Adj. ? H. MERTENS	17, 117, 119, 121, 123
OSTLAND	Königsberg, Oberteichufer 14	OF Reinhold POPPEK Stabsf. OF OHNESORGE	1, 2, 3, 4, 101, 102, 103, 104, 233
OSTSEE	Stettin, Pölitzerstr. 89	OGF ZYNEN ? BF CEDERSTOIPE BF Hans KELLER, m.d.F.b.	7, 8, 9, 10, 108, 111
RHEIN-MOSEL	Koblenz, Steinstr. 23	OF WEIMES WENNER	52, 152, Mb III (?)

NAME (Gruppe)	HQ	COMMANDER	COMPONENT UNITS
SACHSEN	Dresden A, 1, Mosczinskystr. 20	OGF SCHNÜLL OF MÜLLER i.V.	33, 34, 133, 136
SUDETEN (Egerland)	Karlsbad XIII, Adolf-Hitlerstr. 12	BF Helmut JELEN GF Franz MEYER Stabsf. GF PUTZ	200, 201, 202, 203, 204, 205, 206, 207, 208, 209, 210, 211, 212, 213, 214, 215, 313
SÜDWEST	Stuttgart O, Neckarstr. 68	OGF WAGENER SF TRUM	53, 54, 55, 56, 155, 156, 157, 158, 159, Mb4 (?) Mb Staffel "SÜDWEST" (?)
THÜRINGEN	Weimar, Watzdorfstr. 75	GF BARTH	40, 41, 42, 43, 44, 45, 142
WARTHELAND	Posen, Robert Kochstr. 57	GF Paul HOPP	114, 115, 116, 124, 125, 126, 144
WESTFALEN-NORD	Münster	OF WINTER, m.d.F.b.	64, 65, 66, 70
WESTFALEN-SÜD	Dortmund, Kronprinzenstr. 59	OGF Paul NIEDER-WESTERMANN	67, 68, 69
WESTMARK	Kaiserslautern, Lutherstr. 18	GF Rudolf REES (in army)	51, 149, 150, 151, 153, 161, 162, 163, 164, 165, M Staffel "SAAR" (?)
WIEN	Wien III, Metternichg. 4	BF Ernst SCHILLING	93, 94, 193, 194, Mb3 (?)

NAME (Brigade)	HQ	COMMANDER	COMPONENT UNITS
HAMBURG	Hamburg 36, Alsterufer 28	BF Johannes SCHÄDTLER	12, 13
HANSA	Rostock	OGF ZÜNGEL SF FENTZLAFF i.V.	11, 111
KÄRNTEN	Klagenfurt, Hubert Klausner Ring 21	BF HAMMERSCHMID	90, 190
SALZBURG	Salzburg	BF Kurt Günther SECKER	91, 191
SCHWABEN	Augsburg	Ostaf Max BERGMÜLLER	87
STEIERMARK	Graz, Krefelderstr. 31	OF STIEGLER	88, 89, 188
TIROL-VORARLBERG	Innsbruck, Südtirolerplatz 4	SF MAYERBRUCKNER (in army) OF TREIIER (K.F.)	92, 192

PART THREE

NSKK STANDARTEN

NO.	H.Q LOCATION	MOTORGRUPPE	COMMANDER	COMPONENT UNITS
1	Insterburg, Belowstr. 1	OSTLAND		23 M 1 Trempen ? M 1?Memel
2	Allenstein, Treudankstr. 25	OSTLAND		III M 2 Gross Köllen 11 M 2 Schröttersberg 23 M 2 Osterode ? M 2 Plock
3	Elbing, Hindenburgstr.	OSTLAND	SF KARSTEN	1 M 3 Zinten 14 M 3 Pr. Holland 15 M 3 Mühlhausen
4	Königsberg, Gebauhrstr. 16-17	OSTLAND	OF Max HERMSDORF	31 M 4 Königsberg
5	Marienwerder, Hermann-Göring-strasse 6a	DANZIG-Wpr.		26 M 5 Mewe
6	Danzig, Holzmarkt 24	DANZIG-Wpr.	SF KEPPLER	I M 6 Zoppot 5 M 6 Danzig 11 M 6 Gotenhafen 13 M 6 Grabau 22 M 6 Danzig 23 M 6 Danzig 51 M 6 Langfuhr

NO.	HQ LOCATION	MOTORGRUPPE	COMMANDER	COMPONENT UNITS
7	Köslin, Friedrichstr. 20	OSTSEE	SF HOPP	1 M 7 Köslin, Schivelbein 2 M 7 Köslin, Belgard 3 M 7 Köslin 4 M 7 Köslin (Persante?) 13 M 7 Bärwalde 14 M 7 Prechlau
8	Schneidemühl, Mühlenstr. 2	OSTSEE	? SPINDLER	II M 8 Schlönwitz ? 1 M 8 Flatow 2 M 8 Deutsch Krone 4 M 8 Deutsch Krone
9	Stettin, Schulstr. 1	OSTSEE	Ostaff. PETERS	IV M 9 Ueckermünde 4 M 9 Stettin 11 M 9 Stettin 12 M 9 Stettin 13 M 9 Stettin 14 M 9 Stettin 15 M 9 Stettin 25 M 9 Stettin-Politz 34 M 9 Ueckermünde
10	Stralsund, Wasserstr. 79	OSTSEE	SF WACHHOLZ	II M 10 Greifswald 15 M 10 Demmin 16 M 10 Demmin
11	Schwerin i.M., Marstall, Gr. Moor	M.Brig. HANSA	OF REGENSTEIN FENTZLAFF i.V.	I M 11 Schwerin 1 M 11 Schwerin 2 M 11 Schwerin 3 M 11 Schwerin-Wismar 4 M 11 Dassow-Redefin 5 M 11 Wismar 6 M 11 Grevesmühlen 11 M 11 Parchim 13 M 11 Ludwigslust 14 M 11 Eldena 15 M 11 Robel 16 M 11 Malchow 17 M 11 Waren

NO.	HQ LOCATION	MOTORGRUPPE	COMMANDER	COMPONENT UNITS
12	Hamburg Beneckestr. 48	HAMBURG	OF SAND Staff. SAUL i.V.	12 M 12 Hamburg 13 M 12 Hamburg 21 M 12 Hamburg 23 M 12 Hamburg 24 M 12 Hamburg
13	Altona a.Elbe, Flottbecker Chaussee 16	HAMBURG	OF THOMSEN Ostaff. GROTH i.V.	1 M 13 Altona 2 M 13 Altona 3 M 13 Altona 12 M 13 Ulzburg 13 M 13 Elmshorn Hamburg 14 M 13 Barmbeck 15 M 13 Elmshorn 17 M 13 Pinneberg
14	Kiel, Walkerdamm 11, Schifferer-Haus	SCHLESWIG- HOLSTEIN	Ostaff. BLIESCH	I M 14 Malente- Gremsmühlen II M 14 Kiel 2 M 14 Ayrensbök 4 M 14 Lehnsalm 6 M 14 Plön 11 M 14 Kiel 12 M 14 Kiel 13 M 14 Kiel 14 M 14 Eckernförde 15 M 14 Gettorf 16 M 14 Kiel 17 M 14 Kiel 18 M 14 Friedrichsort, Kiel 19 M 14 Kiel
15	Itzehoe, Feldsmiede 98 III	SCHLESWIG- HOLSTEIN	OF. BOYSEN	II M 15 Nortorf III M 15 Wilster 6 M 15 Marne 11 M 15 Rendsburg 13 M 15 Neumünster- Rendsburg 14 M 15 Rendsburg 18 M 15 Kiel 19 M 15 Kiel 22 M 15 30 M 15 Itzehoe

NO.	HQ LOCATION	MOTORGRUPPE	COMMANDER	COMPONENT UNITS
16	Schleswig, Bellmannstr. 19	SCHLESWIG-HOLSTEIN	Staff.O. MÜLLER	3 M 16 Treia 4 M 16 Friedrichskoog 5 M 16 Husum 11 M 16 Flensburg 12 M 16 Langballig 13 M 16 Niebüll 14 M 16 Flensburg 15 M 16 Flensburg
17	Gleiwitz,(O.-S.) Augustastr.10	OBER-SCHLESIEN	? HEINTZE	II M 17 Beuthen 1 M 17 Beuthen 14 M 17 Hindenburg 15 M 17 Beuthen
18	Schweidnitz, Burgstr. 19	NIEDER-SCHLESIEN		13 M 18 Habelschwerdt 21 M 18 Waldenburg
19	Breslau, 13 Strasse der SA.61	NIEDER-SCHLESIEN	Hstuf. JENKE	III M 19 Trebnitz IV M 19 Breslau 31 M 19 Breslau 35 M 19 Breslau 37 M 19 Breslau 41 M 19 Breslau 43 M 19 Breslau 46 M 19 Breslau
20	Unidentified			
21	Liegnitz, Gartenstr. 9	NIEDER-SCHLESIEN		1 M 21 Liegnitz (?) 4 M 21 Liegnitz (?) 12 M 21 Hirschberg 21 M 21 Bunzlau

NO.	HQ LOCATION	MOTORGRUPPE	COMMANDER	COMPONENT UNITS
22	Landsberg, a.Warthe, or Richstr.44	MARK BRANDENBURG		1 M 22 Neudamm 2 M 22 Fürstenwalde Spree 3 M 22 Landesberg 11 M 22 Schwerin
23	Frankfurt a. Oder, Regierungsstr.19	MARK BRANDENBURG		III M 23 Zielenzig 2 M 23 Neudamm 3 M 23 Küstrin 11 M 23 Neudamm 13 M 23 Fürstenwalde 21 M 23 Zielenzig 23 M 23 Fürstenwalde
24	Senftenberg (N.-L.), Schlesischestr 26	MARK BRANDENBURG		
25	Berlin ?	BERLIN		
26	Eberswalde, Eisenbahn-strasse 36	MARK BRANDENBURG		I M 26 Birkenwerder 4 M 26 Glienicke 11 M 26 Zehdenick 23 M 26 Eberswalde 33 M 26 Erkner
27	Potsdam Brandenburger-strasse 62	BERLIN	OSF BASTIAN	III M 27 Luckenwalde IV M 27 Brandenburg 1 M 27 Potsdam 2 M 27 Potsdam 3 M 27 Potsdam 5 M 27 Michendorf 13 M 27 Langesalza 31 M 27 Brandenburg 32 M 27 Brandenburg 33 M 27 Brandenburg
28	Berlin S.W. 68, Zimmerstr. 54	BERLIN	SF FIEDLER	"Ehrensturm Berlin"

NO.	HQ LOCATION	MOTORGRUPPE	COMMANDER	COMPONENT UNITS
29	Berlin W. 57, Potsdamer Str. 92	BERLIN	OSF BOCK	4 M 29 Schönwalde 11 M 29 Spandau 12 M 29 Spandau 14 M 29 Spandau
30	Berlin-Schöneberg Badensche Str. 56 "ERNST VOM RATH"	BERLIN		
31	Berlin S.W. 61, Belle-Alliance-Str. 22	BERLIN	SF. FALK	41 M 31 Berlin-Rudow
32	Berlin ?	BERLIN		42 M 32 Berlin-Wilmersdorf
33	Dresden-A.1 Zinsendorf Str. 4 or Tharander Str. 48 "PAUL LEIN"	SACHSEN	SF. DOMSCH	9 M 33 Dresden 12 M 33 Dresden 21 M 33 Pirna 22 M 33 Dippoldiswalde 23 M 33 Dresden 24 M 33 Possendorf 31 M 33 Pirna 32 M 33 Königstein 41 M 33 Dresden

NO.	HQ LOCATION	MOTORGRUPPE	COMMANDER	COMPONENT UNITS
34	Chemnitz, Further Trift 11	SACHSEN		IV M 34 Annaberg-Buchholz 1 M 34 Chemnitz 2 M 34 Gersdorf 3 M 34 Chemnitz 4 M 34 Chemnitz 5 M 34 Chemnitz 6 M 34 Chemnitz 11 M 34 Chemnitz 12 M 34 Chemnitz 13 M 34 Chemnitz 14 M 34 Chemnitz 15 M 34 Chemnitz 21 M 34 Annaberg-Buchholz, Frankenberg 22 M 34 Flöha 24 M 34 Zschopau 32 M 34 Annaberg-Buchholz 33 M 34 Annaberg-Buchholz 34 M 34 Ehrenfriedersdorf 36 M 34 Annaberg-Buchholz 42 M 34 Marienberg 51 M 34 Limbach 52 M 34 Chemnitz 53 M 34 Neunkirchen (Erzgeb.) 61 M 34 Freiberg 62 M 34 Freiberg
35	Leipzig, C.1, Otto Schiller Strasse 3/5	LEIPZIG	OF WEIDLICH	I M 35 Leipzig II M 35 Leipzig III M 35 Leipzig 1 M 35 Leipzig 2 M 35 Leipzig 3 M 35 Leipzig 4 M 35 Leipzig 5 M 35 Leipzig 6 M 35 Leipzig 11 M 35 Leipzig 12 M 35 Leipzig 13 M 35 Leipzig 14 M 35 Leipzig 15 M 35 Leipzig 21 M 35 Leipzig 22 M 35 Leipzig 24 M 35 Leipzig

NO.	HQ LOCATION	MOTORGRUPPE	COMMANDER	COMPONENT UNITS
36	Plauen 1, Vogtland, Adolf-Hitler-Str. 56 or Schneeberg Hindenburgplatz 153	LEIPZIG		III M 36 Oelsnitz, Adorf, Niederwiesa & Flöha IV M 36 Falkenstein 1 M 36 Zwickau 2 M 36 Zwickau 3 M 36 Zwickau 4 M 36 Reichenbach 7 M 36 Reichenbach 8 M 36 Zwickau 9 M 36 Zwickau 10 M 36 Zwickau 11 M 36 Schneeberg 12 M 36 Aue 13 M 36 Zschorlau 14 M 36 Schwarzenberg 15 M 36 Johanngeorgenstadt 22 M 36 Ölsnitz 23 M 36 Ölsnitz 32 M 36 Auerbach 33 M 36 Treuen 34 M 36 Klingenthal
37	Torgau a. Elbe. Mühlen Str. 5	LEIPZIG	O STAFF GEORG KUNSEKE	I M 37 Wittenberg IV M 37 Ortrand 12 M 37 Bockwitz
38	Halle-Saale Konig. Str. 58	LEIPZIG		I M 38 Halle/Saale II M 38 Halle/Saale III M 38 Grafenhainchen 1 M 38 Halle/Saale 2 M 38 Halle/Saale 3 M 38 Halle/Saale 4 M 38 Halle/Saale 5 M 38 Halle/Saale 6 M 38 Halle/Saale 11 M 38 Halle/Saale 12 M 38 Halle/Saale 14 M 38 Halle/Saale 21 M 38 Grafenhainchen 31 M 38 Eilenburg 32 M 38 Delitzsch

NO.	HQ LOCATION	MOTORGRUPPE	COMMANDER	COMPONENT UNITS
39	Halberstadt, Mahndorfer Str.20	LEIPZIG	OF STICHERLING	III M 39 Magdeburg 1 M 39 Halberstadt 4 M 39 Halberstadt 6 M 39 Halberstadt 15 M 39 Magdeburg 21 M 39 Magdeburg/Wernigerode 24 M 39 Blankenburg
40	Watenstedt-Salzgitter, Ortsteil Lebenstedt	THÜRINGEN	Ostaff. KAUTZ	12 M 40 Magdeburg
41	Gera, Adolf-Hitler-Platz 4	THÜRINGEN	SF STRACENY	4 M 41 Weida
42	Weimar, Watzdorf Str.73	THÜRINGEN		II M 42 Apolda 15 M 42 Apolda 18 M 42 Apolda 22 M 42 Eckartsberge
43	Rudolstadt, Katharinastr.30, Schliessfach 162	THÜRINGEN		1 M 43 Arnstadt ? 2 M 43 Arnstadt ? 3 M 43 Stadtilm 11 M 43 Rudolstadt 12 M 43 Possneck 21 M 43 Zella-Mehlis
44	Eisenach, Karlstr. 1	THÜRINGEN		I M 44 Ohrdorf II M 44 Meiningen IV M 44 Esslingen 1 M 44 Gotha 3 M 44 Zella-Mehlis 5 M 44 Ohrdruf 8 M 44 Zella-Mehlis 11 M 44 Hildenhausen

NO.	HQ LOCATION	MOTORGRUPPE	COMMANDER	COMPONENT UNITS
45	Nordhausen, Neustadtstr. 9	THÜRINGEN		III M 45 Kölleda 2 M 45 Mühlhausen 5 M 45 Bleicherode 12 M 45 Nordhausen 14 M 45 Sonderhausen 24 M 45 Sangerhausen
46	Hanau a.M., Mühltorweg 3	HESSEN		III M 46 Friedberg 11 M 46 Fulda 12 M 46 Fulda
47	Kassel, Bahnhofstr. 2	HESSEN	SF OPPEL OSF FRIEDRICHS i.V.	1 M 47 Kassel 2 M 47 Kassel 3 M 47 Kassel 4 M 47 Kassel 5 M 47 Kassel 6 M 47 Kassel 12 M 47 Kassel 13 M 47 Langensalzen 15 M 47 Hann. Minden 31 M 47 Eschwege 34 M 47 Hersfeld 43 M 47 Hann. Minden
48	Marburg/Lahn, Frankfurter Str. 53 or Barfüsser Str. 1	hESSEN		I M 48 Marburg II M 48 Frankenberg/Eder III M 48 Frankenberg/Eder 1 M 48 Marburg 2 M 48 Marburg 3 M 48 Marburg 4 M 48 Marburg 11 M 48 Frankenberg/Eder 13 M 48 Korbach 22 M 48 Bad Wildungen ? M 48?Liesen I K 48 Marburg II K 48 Bad Wildungen III K 48 Korbach 1 K 48 Marburg 21 K 48 Korbach 22 K 48 Frankenberg/Eder
49	Frankfurt a.Main, Kettenhofweg 55	HESSEN	SBF BACKHAUSEN	III M 49 Langen 1 M 49 2 M 49 Frankfurt a.M. 5 M 49 Frankfurt a.M. 7 M 49 Frankfurt a.M. 8 M 49 Frankfurt a.M. 11 M 49 Frankfurt a.M. 12 M 49 Bad Hamburg 21 M 49 Frankfurt a.M. 22 M 49 Frankfurt a.M. 23 M 49 Frankfurt a.M. 24 M 49 Frankfurt a.M.

NO.	HQ. LOCATION	MOTORGRUPPE	COMMANDER	COMPONENT UNITS
50	Darmstadt, Alexanderweg 6	HESSEN		III M 50 Reichelsheim IV M 50 Heppenheim 23 M 50 Michelstadt
51	Ludwigshafen a. Rhein, Oberes Rheinufer 33	WESTMARK		11 M 51 Speyer 12 M 51 Neustadt/Weinstrasse 22 M 51 Frankenthal 23 M 51 Pirmasens
52	Neuwied a. Rhein, Dierdorfer Str. 203	RHEIN MOSEL		II M 52 Neuwied 14 M 52 Aschersleben
53	Karlsruhe Kriegsstr. 29	SÜDWEST	SF HAMPE	I M 53 Karlsruhe II M 53 Pforzheim III M 53 Gaggenau 3 M 53 Karlsruhe 7 M 53 Durlach 22 M 53 Rastatt 23 M 53 Rastatt or Baden-Baden 24 M 53 Schramberg 32 M 53 Offenburg 33 M 53 Offenburg
54	Freiburg i. Br., Maria-Theresia-strasse 2	SÜDWEST	SF KLEMM	IV M 54 Rümmingen 1 M 54 Freiburg 3 M 54 Freiburg 9 M 54 Freiburg 11 M 54 Villingen 12 M 54 Donau-Eschingen 13 M 54 Triberg 15 M 54 Rottweil 31 M 54 Rümmingen 32 M 54 Lörrach 33 M 54 Schopfheim 41 M 54 Emmendingen

NO.	HQ. LOCATION	MOTORGRUPPE	COMMANDER	COMPONENT UNITS
55	Stuttgart-S, Filderstr. 45, Postschliessfach 370	SÜDWEST	SF KLAUS AUKTOR	I M 55 Stuttgart II M 55 Ludwigsburg III M 55 Filder IV M 55 Eschingen V M 55 Tübingen 1 M 55 Stuttgart 2 M 55 Stuttgart 3 M 55 Stuttgart 4 M 55 Cannstadt 5 M 55 Feuerbach 6 M 55 Stuttgart 7 M 55 Stuttgart 23 M 55 Herrenberg 31 M 55 Eschingen 32 M 55 Eschingen 35 M 55 Feldbach 41 M 55 Tübingen 42 M 55 Tübingen 43 M 55 Tübingen 46 M 55 Reutlingen 47 M 55 Tübingen ? M 55 Fürstenfeld
56	Ulm a. Donau, Grüner Hof. 5	SÜDWEST	SF HAICHBRONNER	IV M 56 Heidenheim, Reutlingen V M 56 Tübingen 7 M 56 Laupheim 12 M 56 Göppingen 31 M 56 Reutlingen 32 M 56 Reutlingen 34 M 56 Wendlingen 41 M 56 Tübingen 43 M 56 Tübingen 44 M 56 Tübingen 47 M 56 Tübingen
57	Göttingen, Litzmannstr. 1a	NIEDER SACHSEN		12 M 57 Osterode 14 M 57 Northeim 15 M 57 Moringen 22 M 57 Ottenstein
58	Braunschweig, Leonhardplatz 11	NIEDER SACHSEN		1 M 58 Braunschweig 2 M 58 Braunschweig 5 M 58 Flechtorf 23 M 58 Schonin 24 M 58 Helmstedt

NO.	HQ. LOCATION	MOTORGRUPPE	COMMANDER	COMPONENT UNITS
59	Hildesheim Hermann-Römer-Str. 3	NIEDER-SACHSEN		II M 59 Peine III M 59 Goslar IV M 59 Holzminden 21 M 59 Bad Harzburg
60	Ülzen i. Hannover, Adolf-Hitler-strasse 5	NIEDER-SACHSEN		II M 60 Ülzen III M 60 Celle 11 M 60 Ebstorf 21 M 60 Celle 31 M 60 Ebstorf 34 M 60 Fallersleben
61	Hannover, Hohenzollernstr. 42	NIEDER-SACHSEN		II M 61 Hameln 11 M 61 Hameln 12 M 61 Rinteln 18 M 61 Bückeburg 26 M 61 Blankenburg
62	Bremen, Delbrückstr. 18 or Wachstrasse 27	NORDSEE	? LEHMANN	1 M 62 Wesermünde 2 M 62 Wesermünde 11 M 62 15 M 62 Bremen 16 M 62 Bremen 17 M 62 Verden 21 M 62 Nienburg/Weser 22 M 62 Hoya
63	Oldenburg, Auguststr. 4	NORDSEE	SF WIEDER	I M 63 Vechta III M 63 Delmenhorst 1 M 63 Oldenburg 2 M 63 Oldenburg 4 M 63 Bad Zwischenahn 5 M 63 Berga 7 M 63 Wilhelmshafen 8 M 63 Varel 9 M 63 Neuharlingersiel 12 M 63 Marienhafen 13 M 63 Wittmund 17 M 63 Wilhelmshafen 18 M 63 Leer 21 M 63 Delmenhorst 24 M 63 Vechta 25 M 63 Cloppenburg 26 M 63 Delmenhorst 31 M 63 Leer

NO.	HQ. LOCATION	MOTORGRUPPE	COMMANDER	COMPONENT UNITS
64	Osnabrück Seminarstr. 32	WESTFALEN NORD	Hstuf. KÖRNER	I M 64 Osnabrück II M 64 Minden 1 M 64 Osnabrück(?) 3 M 64 Melle 5 M 64 Berge 6 M 64 Osnabrück(?) 11 M 64 Minden 13 M 64 Lübbecke 14 M 64 Herford 24 M 64 Papenburg
65	Bielefeld, Hindenburgstr. 13	WESTFALEN NORD		I M 65 Bielefeld II M 65 Paderborn 1 M 65 Bielefeld 2 M 65 Bielefeld 3 M 65 Gütersloh 4 M 65 Halle 7 M 65 Schötmar-Salzuflen 11 M 65 Paderborn 12 M 65 Büren 14 M 65 Bad Lippspringe
66	Münster, i.Westf., Krummestr. 10	WESTFALEN NORD	SF HAUNEFORTH	I M 66 Münster I M 66 Münster 2 M 66 Münster 3 M 66 Münster 4 M 66 Münster 7 M 66 Neubeckum 8 M 66 Beckum 11 M 66 Coesfeld 13 M 66 Münster 21 M 66 Bocholt 34 M 66 Bottrop
67	Dortmund II. Kampstr. 3	WESTFALEN SÜD	Ostaff DAUBER, m.d.F.b.	1 M 67 Dortmund 2 M 67 Dortmund 7 M 67 Dortmund 12 M 67 Hamm 13 M 67 Hamm 14 M 67 Unna 21 M 67 Soest 22 M 67 Soest 23 M 67 Lippstadt 53 M 67 Dortmund
68	Arnsberg i. Westf., Hermann-Goring-Str. 22	WESTFALEN SÜD		6 M 68 Brilon 11 M 68 Werdohl 12 M 68 Ludenscheid 13 M 68 Altena 14 M 68 Hohenlimburg 23 M 68 Schwerte 25 M 68 Menden

NO.	HQ. LOCATION	MOTORGRUPPE	COMMANDER	COMPONENT UNITS
69	Bochum, Neustr. 22	WESTFALEN SÜD	? RÖCKERS- HAUSEN	I M 69 Hattingen II M 69 Bochum 3 M 69 Gevelsburg 11 M 69 Bochum 12 M 69 Bochum 16 M 69 Bochum 17 M 69 Bochum 18 M 69 Witter 21 M 69 Wanne-Eickel 22 M 69 Wanne-Eickel 23 M 69 Herne 24 M 69 Castrop-Rauxel 25 M 69 Castrop-Rauxel
70	Gelsenkirchen, Dietrich-Eckart-strasse 9	WESTFALEN NORD		1 M 70 Gelsenkirchen 2 M 70 Gelsenkirchen 3 M 70 Bottrop 4 M 70 Gladbeck 5 M 70 Gelsenkirchen
71	Köln a.Rhein, Kaesenstr. 4	NIEDERRHEIN		I M 71 Köln 8 M 71 Köln 11 M 71 Bonn 12 M 71 Bonn 15 M 71 Bonn
72	Wuppertal-Elberfeld, Strasse der SA 117	NIEDERRHEIN	? RUPPERT	3 M 72 Wuppertal 5 M 72 Velbert 7 M 72 Hilden
73	Essen, Bismarck-strasse 27	NIEDERRHEIN		2 M 73 Mühlheim 11 M 73 Oberhausen

NO.	HQ. LOCATION	MOTORGRUPPE	COMMANDER	COMPONENT UNITS
74	Duisburg, Düsseldorfer-str. 102	NIEDERRHEIN		II M 74 Wesel 3 M 74 Duisburg 12 M 74 Kevelaer 14 M 74 Viersen
75	Düsseldorf, NSKK - Baracke Staufenplatz "ALBERT SCHNEIDER"	NIEDERRHEIN	SF GETHMANN	I M 75 Düsseldorf II M 75 Krefeld III M 75 Rheydt München-Gladbach 8 M 75 Düsseldorf 9 M 75 Düsseldorf 14 M 75 Viersen 21 M 75 München/Gladbach 22 M 75 München/Gladbach 23 M 75 Rheydt 26 M 75 Rheydt 27 M 75 Greven
76	Aachen Kaiserplatz 9	NIEDERRHEIN	OSF Pg. GÜNKEL? HSF HERMANNS i.V.	I M 76 Aachen II M 76 Aachen 1 M 76 Aachen 2 M 76 Aachen 3 M 76 Aachen 4 M 76 Aachen 23 M 76 Moresnet
77	Bayreuth, Richard-Wagner Strasse 6	BAYERNWALD		IV M 77 Selbitz V M 77 Wunsiedl 11 M 77 Weiden 14 M 77 Coburg 15 M 77 Hof 26 M 77 Schwanhof 35 M 77 Hof 41 M 77 Stopfersfurth 43 M 77 Marktredwitz
78	Ansbach, Adolf Hitler-Platz 8	FRANKEN		I M 78 Bad Mergentheim 2 M 78 Weikersheim 3 M 78 Künzelsau 12 M 78 Crailsheim

NO.	HQ LOCATION	MOTORGRUPPE	COMMANDER	COMPONENT UNITS
79	Schweinfurt Adolf-Hitler-Strasse 9	FRANKEN	OF KUHR	II M 79 Würzburg 1. M 79 Schweinfurt ?
80	Landshut, Untere Schwimmschulstr. 1	BAYERNWALD		14 M 80 Vilshofen
81	Regensburg, Dr.-Martin-Luther-Str. 14/0	BAYERNWALD	Ostaff. KERSCHENSTEINER i.V.	24 M 81 Regensburg
82	Amberg	BAYERNWALD		3 M 82 Vilseck
83	Nürnberg, Further St.10 I	FRANKEN	OF. HORNDRASCH	12 M 83 Altdorf 13 M 83 Schwabach 32 M 83 Fürth 33 M 83 Fürth 39 M 83 Erlangen
84	Rosenheim, Alolf-Hitler-Strasse 3 1/3 "KOLBERMOOR"	HÜHNLEIN	OSF ELLWANGER	12 M 84 Traunstein 13 M 84 Bad Reichenhall
85	Weilheim, Oberbayern Münchner Strasse 30	HÜHNLEIN		II M 85 Garmisch-Partenkirchen 2 M 85 Garmisch-Partenkirchen 6 M 85 Augsburg 15 M 85 Lindau

NO.	HQ LOCATION	MOTORGRUPPE	COMMANDER	COMPONENT UNITS
86	München 2, Herzog-Wilhelm-Strasse 13	HÜHNLEIN	SF ZIMMERMANN Staff. HELLER i.V.	4 M 86 München 5 M 86 München 8 M 86 München 10 M 86 München 13 M 86 München 17 M 86 München 26 M 86 München
87	Augsburg, Frauentor-Str. 25/II Reg.	Brig. SCHWABEN	Ostaff. Max BERGMÜLLER	16 M 87 Donauwörth
88	Graz, Girardigasse 1 "SIEGFRIED SCHOTT"	Brig. STEIERMARK		I M 88 Graz II M 88 Graz 1 M 88 Graz 2 M 88 Graz 3 M 88 Graz 4 M 88 Graz 5 M 88 Graz 6 M 88 Graz 7 M 88 Graz 8 M 88 Graz 11 M 88 Graz 12 M 88 Graz 13 M 88 Graz, Feldbach 14 M 88 Graz 15 M 88 Graz 16 M 88 Graz 17 M 88 Graz 21 M 88 Köflach, Knittelfeld 23 M 88 Graz ? M 88 ?Fürstenfeld
89	Leoben, Sauragasse, 1/II "JOHANN SCHNEER"	Brig. STEIERMARK		2 M 89 Kapfenberg 25 M 89 Neudau ? M 89 ?Schladming

NO.	HQ LOCATION	MOTORGRUPPE	COMMANDER	COMPONENT UNITS	
90	Klagenfurt, Viktringer-ring 2 "ARTUR SEEBER"	Brig. KÄRNTEN	SF Kurt WAGNER	III M 90 Klagenfurt V M 90 Krainsburg	
91	Salzburg Kaigasse 39/I "ALFRED JANKE"	Brig. SALZBURG		23 M 91 Zellamsee 25 M 91 Markt Pongau 26 M 91 Werfen 27 M 91 Tannheim	
92	Innsbruck Südtiroler-platz 4	Brig. TIROL	OF Eugen WILLAM	I M 92 Innsbruck II M 92 Innsbruck III M 92 Wörgl 5 M 92 Innsbruck 13 M 92 Telfs 14 M 92 Reutte 22 M 92 Kitzbühel 24 M 92 Jenbach 25 M 92 Schwaz 26 M 92 Mayrhofen ? M 92 or 192 Feldkirch	
93	Wien 18, Wahringer-gürtel 40	Wien	Staff von der CASTEL	I M 93 Wien II M 93 Wien III M 93 Wien IV M 93 Wien V M 93 Wien 1 M 93 Wien 2 M 93 Wien 3 M 93 Wien 4 M 93 Wien 5 M 93 Wien 6 M 93 Wien 7 M 93 Wien 11 M 93 Wien 14 M 93 Wien 15 M 93 Wien 16 M 93 Wien 17 M 93 Wien 21 M 93 Wien 22 M 93 Wien 23 M 93 Wien 24 M 93 Wien 25 M 93 Wien 26 M 93 Wien 31 M 93 Wien 32 M 93 Wien 33 M 93 Wien	V/55 I/1 IX/71 I/1 VI/56 VI/56 VI/56 VII/62 VIII/65 IX/66 IX/66 IX/71 IX/71 III/40 III/40 III/40 III/40 III/40 III/40 IV/50 IV/50 IV/50

NO.	HQ LOCATION	MOTORGRUPPE	COMMANDER	COMPONENT UNITS	
93	Wien (Cont.)	WIEN		34 M 93 Wien	IV/50
				35 M 93 Wien	V/55
				36 M 93 Wien	V/55
				37 M 93 Wien	V/55
94	Wien 110, 18 Bezirk, Hasenauer Str. 63	WIEN		I M 94 Wien	XVI/107
				II M 94 Wien	XV/101
				IV M 94 Wien	XVII/107
				V M 94 Wien	XIX/117
				1 M 94 Wien	XVI(XI?)/107
				2 M 94 Wien	XVI(XI?)/107
				3 M 94 Wien	XVI/107
				4 M 94 Wien	XVI/107
				5 M 94 Wien	XVI/107
				11 M 94 Wien	XV/101
				12 M 94 Wien	XV/101
				13 M 94 Wien	XV/101
				21 M 94 Wien	XIV/89
				23 M 94 Wien-Punkersdorf	XIV
				24 M 94 Wien	VII/62
				31 M 94 Wien	XVII/107
				32 M 94 Wien	XVII/107
				33 M 94 Wien	XVIII/107
				34 M 94 Wien	XVIII/110
				42 M 94 Wien	XIX/117
				43 M 94 Wien-Klosterneuburg	XXVI
95	Coburg, ob. Burglass 9	FRANKEN	SF LIMKE		
96	Krems, Heinemannstr. 5	NIEDERDONAU	SF MEHRL	2 M 96 Stockerau	
				13 M 96 Laa/Thaya	
				15 M 96 Retz	
				22 M 96 Korneuburg	
				33 M 96 Horn	
				34 M 96 Langenlois	
				45 M 96 Zwettel	
				? M 96 ?Gänserndorf	

NO.	HQ LOCATION	MOTORGRUPPE	COMMANDER	COMPONENT UNITS
97	Eisenstadt Oberberg, 178, Postfach 83	NIEDER-DONAU	SF EICHEN-SEDER	31 M 97 Liesing 32 M 97 Perchtoldsdorf 33 M 97 Liesing 62 M 97 Ternitz ? M 97?Asparn an der Zaya ? M 97?Baden
98	St. Pölten, Nieder-Donau, Rossmarkt 1a	NIEDER-DONAU		
99	Linz a. Donau, Landstr. 36	OBER-DONAU		2 M 99 Perg 13 M 99 Leonding-Paschitz 32 M 99 Waizen-Kirchen ? M 99?Wels
100	Gmünden, Ob. Donau, Hochmüllergasse 11	OBER-DONAU	SF HEIBLER	I M 100 Steyr 3 M 100 Steyr 14 M 100 Kirchdorf/Krems 32 M 100 Gmünden 99 M 100 Braunau am Inn. ? M 100?Wels
101	Lötzen, Hindenburgstrasse 1	OST-LAND	SF SCHEUNL i.V.	
102	Rastenburg, Ordensschloss	OSTLAND		13 M 102 Friedland 26 M 102 Pr. Holland

NO.	HQ LOCATION	MOTORGRUPPE	COMMANDER	COMPONENT UNITS
103	Insterburg or Tilsit, Hohe Str. 42, I.	OSTLAND		III M 103 Ahrens 6 M 103 Heydekrug 7 M 103 Kirschheim-Teck 25 M 103 Pr. Mark 26 M 103 Insterburg, Heydekrug
104	Tilsit ? Hohe Str. 42, I (?)	OSTLAND		
105	Thorn, Hermann-Göring-Str.104	DANZIG WPR.		
106	Bromberg, Weltzien-platz 1	DANZIG WPR.	Ostaff HENKEL HENKEL	3 M 106 Bromberg 4 M 106
107	Stolp i. Pr., Hindenburg-str. 44	OSTSEE		12 M 107 Hammerstein
108	Stargard, Heilige Geiststr. 19	OSTSEE		II M 108 Swinemünde 4 M 108 Pyritz, Anklam 11 M 108 Greifenberg 12 M 108 Wollin 14 M 108 Anklam

NO.	HQ LOCATION	MOTORGRUPPE	COMMANDER	COMPONENT UNITS
111	Rostock i. Mecklb., Bucherplatz 1/L "OSTMECKLENBURG"	Brig. HANSA	OF REGENSTEIN Ostaff. PAULSEN i.V.	I M 111 Rostock 1 M 111 Rostock 2 M 111 Rostock 3 M 111 Rostock 4 M 111 Rostock, Ribnitz 5 M 111 Rostock 13 M 111 Güstrow 14 M 111 Bützow 15 M 111 Güstrow 22 M 111 Neubrandenburg 31 M 111 Robel 32 M 111 Malchow 42 M 111 Dargon 43 M 111 Bad Doberan 44 M 111 Liebnitz 53 M 111 Rostock
112	Neuruppin, Fehrbelliner Str. 5	BRANDENBURG	Staff. SCHÜTZE	1 M 112 Parchin 3 M 112 Neustadt 4 M 112 Rathenow 5 M 112 Rathenow, Kyritz 12 M 112 Wittenberge 15 M 112 Kyritz 22 M 112 Kremmen 23 M 112 Nauen 24 M 112 Falkensee
113	Lübeck Werftstr. 2	SCHLESWIG-HOLSTEIN	SF LEPTIEN	I M 113 Lübeck 2 M 113 Barmstedt "Martin Tiessen" 5 M 113 Mölin, Mollhagen 12 M 113 Heidmühlen bei Neumünster 24 M 113 Heidrege 25 M 113 Pinneberg
114	Posen, Richard-Wagner-Str. 2	WARTHELAND	HSF MÜLLER	V M 114 Kolmar 2 M 114 Posen 31 M 114 Samter

NO.	HQ LOCATION	MOTORGRUPPE	COMMANDER	COMPONENT UNITS
115	Hohensalza, Bahnhofstr. 21	WARTHELAND		III M 115 Leslau IV M 115 Kutno 3 M 115 Sperlingshof 21 M 115 Leslau
116	Litzmannstadt Adolf-Hitler-Str. 53	WARTHELAND	OF HEYDENREICH i.V. Ostaff. BÜCHLER	V M 116 Pabianice 1 M 116 Litzmannstadt 15 M 116 Litzmannstadt 22 M 116 Schieratz
117	Oppeln, i. Sches., Zimmerstr. 4	OBER-SCHLESIEN	HSF KIESE-WETTER i.V. Staff. WODAK	4 M 117 Neisse 11 M 117 Kreuzburg 12 M 117 Rosenberg 13 M 117 Strelitz 21 M 117 Neustadt/O.S. 23 M 117 Leobschutz
118	Görlitz, Bei der Peterskirche 12	NIEDER SCHLESIEN	OSF Kurt STEMMLER m.d.F.b.	1 M 118 Sprottau 2 M 118 Rothenburg 3 M 118 Freiwaldau 4 M 118 Sagau 11 M 118 Görlitz 12 M 118 Görlitz 15 M 118 Lauban 16 M 118 Lauban 17 M 118 Kohlfurt 27 M 118 Hoyerswerda
119	Kattowitz, Ludendorff-Ecke Kalide-Str., Bar. 23	OBER-SCHLESIEN		1 M 119 Kattowitz 2 M 119 Kattowitz 3 M 119 Schoppinitz 4 M 119 Myslowitz 5 M 119 Kattowitz 6 M 119 Königshutte-Laurahütte 8 M 119 Myslenice 9 M 119 Bendsburg 11 M 119 Königshütte 12 M 119 Bismarckhütte 13 M 119 Morgenroth/Ruda 14 M 119 Friedenshütte 15 M 119 Antonienhütte 16 M 119 Bielosowicz 17 M 119 Liepine 21 M 119 Tarnowitz 22 M 119 Bobrownik 23 M 119 Stahlhammer 24 M 119 Nakle 25 M 119 Azarlej 26 M 119 Loeben

NO.	HQ LOCATION	MOTORGRUPPE	COMMANDER	COMPONENT UNITS
120	Glogau, Langestr. 28	NIEDER-SCHLESIEN		1 M 120 Guhrau 11 M 120 Glogau 12 M 120 Glogau
121	Kattowitz, Ludendorff-Ecke Kalide-Str., Bar.23	OBER-SCHLESIEN	SF WODAK	I M 121 Teschen II M 121 Bielitz III M 121 Bielitz 3 M 121 Teschen 14 M 121 Auschwitz 22 M 121 Nikolei 27 M 121 Tichau
122	Guben, Herrenstr. 16	BRANDENBURG		I M 122 Züllichen 3 M 122 Sorau 5 M 122 Linderode 21 M 122 Cottbus 24 M 122 Cottbus
123	Krakau, 1, Weichselstr. 5., Postfach 1090	OBER-SCHLESIEN		
124	Lissa, Lindenstr. 42	WARTHELAND		V M 124 Wroschen 1 M 124 Lissa 12 M 124 Krotoschin 25 M 124 Friedenhorst 42 M 124 Jarotschin
125	Gnesen, Trenessener-str. 33	WARTHELAND		24 M 125 Dietfurt 38 M 125 Warthebrück

NO.	HQ LOCATION	MOTORGRUPPE	COMMANDER	COMPONENT UNITS
126	Kalisch, Hermann-Göring-Str. 17	WARTHELAND		15 M 126 Welungen 23 M 126 Welungen
130	Bromberg	DANZIG-WPR.		
133	Zittau i. Sa., Bahnofstr. 15	SACHSEN		II M 133 Bischofswerda 1 M 133 Zittau 2 M 133 Neugersdorf 11 M 133 Bautzen 12 M 133 Kirschau 21 M 133 Warnsdorf 22 M 133 Warnsdorf 23 M 133 Warnsdorf 24 M 133 Schönlinde Kr. Rumburg 25 M 133 Rumburg 26 M 133 Georgswalde 29 M 133 Grossschönau "Nixdorf"
135	Dessau, Ruststr. 1	MAGDEBURG-ANHALT		III M 135 Dessau 1 M 135 Dessau 2 M 135 Dessau 3 M 135 Dessau 5 M 135 Dessau 7 M 135 Magdeburg 13 M 135 Hecklingen
136	Zwickau, Platz der SA.6	SACHSEN	SF KUNZ	4 M 136 Zwickau 5 M 136 Werdau 6 M 136 Crimmitschau 11 M 136 Lichtenstein 14 M 136 Glauchau 15 M 136 Hohenstein-Ernstthal
137	Magdeburg, Göringstr. 18a	NIEDER-SACHSEN or LEIPZIG	Staff. FANGER	III M 137 Biederitz bei Magdeburg IV M 137 Schöneck bei Magdeburg 2 M 137 Magdeburg 3 M 137 Magdeburg 4 M 137 Magdeburg 5 M 137 Magdeburg 6 M 137 Magdeburg

NO.	HQ. LOCATION	MOTORGRUPPE	COMMANDER	COMPONENT UNITS
137	Magdeburg, (cont.) Göringstr. 18a	NIEDER-SACHSEN or LEIPZIG		10 M 137 Magdeburg 12 M 137 Magdeburg 25 M 137 Wittstook 35 M 137 Hecklingen 41 M 137 Magdeburg 42 M 137 Magdeburg 44 M 137 Magdeburg 51 M 137 Magdeburg 52 M 137 Magdeburg 53 M 137 Magdeburg 54 M 137 Magdeburg 55 M 137 Magdeburg 56 M 137 Magdeburg
138	Weissenfels a.Sa.Le, Zeiter Str. 78, Haus der NSKK	NIEDER-SACHSEN		2 M 138 Weissenfels 3 M 138 Naumburg 4 M 138 Naumburg 15 M 138 Naumburg
141	Mittweida i.Sa., Max-Beulich Str. 19	LEIPZIG		I M 141 Wurzen III M 141 Altenburg 2 M 141 Wurzen 3 M 141 Oschatz 13 M 141 Waldheim 15 M 141 Burgstadt 17 M 141 Mittweida 21 M 141 Burgstadt 22 M 141 Altenburg
142	Erfurt, Dalbergsweg 30	THURINGEN	SF BERNHARDT	II M 142 Erfurt III M 142 Erfurt 1 m 142 Erfurt 4 M 142 Erfurt 5 M 142 Erfurt 6 M 142 Erfurt 11 M 142 Bad Temstedt 13 M 142 Langensalza 22 M 142 Erfurt 23 M 142 Erfurt 24 M 142 Weimar
146	Aschaffenburg, Treibgasse 24	HESSEN	SF Peter HENSS	I M 146 Hersfeld 1 M 146 Hersfeld 3 M 146 Aschaffenburg(?) 23 M 146 Michelstadt I K 146 Hersfeld 1 K 146 Hersfeld 2 K 146 Rotenburg

NO.	HQ. LOCATION	MOTORGRUPPE	COMMANDER	COMPONENT UNITS
147	Giessen, Frankfurter Str. 33	HESSEN		II M 147 Lauterbach 1 M 147 Giessen 2 M 147 Gross Linden 4 M 147 Giessen 12 M 147 Alsfeld 14 M 147 Grünberg
148	Wiesbaden Langssee 9	HESSEN		
149	Luxemburg, Liebfrauenstr. 42	WESTMARK	SF SCHWÄMLEIN	6 M 149 Steinfurt
150	Mainz, Kaiserstr. 30	WESTMARK		II M 150 Burgen III M 150 Worms
151	Kaiserslautern, Dr-Martin-Luther-Str. 18	WESTMARK		1 M 151 Kaiserslautern 2 M 151 Kaiserslautern 4 M 151 Landstuhl 13 M 151 Homburg/Saar 31 M 151 Kaiserslautern 32 M 151 Kaiserslautern
152	Trier Thyrusstr. 45, Goetenkaserne	RHEIN-MOSEL	Ostaff. KAISER	II M 152 Idar-Oberstein III M 152 Daun 1 M 152 Trier 2 M 152 Trier 3 M 152 Trier 11 M 152 Idar-Oberstein 21 M 152 Koblenz
153	Heidelberg, Neue Schloss-str. 7	WESTMARK	SF ZIERENBERG	I M 153 Mannheim 12 M 153 Heidelberg 15 M 153 Sinzheim 21 M 153 Seckenheim 23 M 153 Weinheim

NO.	HQ. LOCATION	MOTORGRUPPE	COMMANDER	COMPONENT UNITS
154	Hagenau in Elsass, Strassburgerstr. 3A			1 M 154 Hagenau 2 M 154 Hagenau
155	Heilbronn, a. Neckar Dittmarstr. 16	SÜDWEST	OF HARZER SF AUKTOR/KF	2 M 155 Neckarsulm 4 M 155 Lauffen, Heilbronn 11 M 155 Heilbronn 32 M 155 Würzburg
156	Konstanz a. Bodensee, Adolf-Hitler-Ufer 9	SÜDWEST	SF KLEMM	III M 156 Sigmaringen 1 M 156 Trossingen 3 M 156 Überlingen 14 M 156 Friedrichshafen 22 M 156 Jungingen 32 M 156 Saulgau
157	Strassburg Neuweilerhofstaden 6	SÜDWEST	SF SEIGEL ? HUBER	2 M 157 Strassburg 5 M 157 Bischheim 12 M 157 Strassburg 14 M 157 Neudorf 15 M 157 Königshofen
158	Kolmar, Schlumbergerstr. 11	SÜDWEST	SF HUBER	6 M 158 Kaysersberg 15 M 158 Kaysersberg 21 M 158 Gebweiler
159	Mülhausen, (Mulhouse) Kamispfad 35	SÜDWEST	Hstuf. Walter RUDOLPH	
160	Lüneburg Am Benedikt 10	NORDSEE	SF ÖCKERS	1 M 160 Lüneburg 6 M 160 Munster-Lager 11 M 160 Stade 12 M 160 Stade 14 M 160 Cuxhaven 15 M 160 Neuhaus

NO.	HQ. LOCATION	MOTORGRUPPE	COMMANDER	COMPONENT UNITS
161	Diedenhofen, Bergschulstr. 30	WESTMARK	OF LECKEBUSCH	1 M 161 Niederjeutz(?) 2 M 161 Diedenhofen 7 M 161 Diedenhofen
162	Metz, Bismarckstr. 12	RHEIN-MOSEL	SF GETHMANN SS. BF DUNKERN	II M 162 Diedenhofen. III M 162 Rombach 12 M 162 Deutscho ? 1.L. (in Lothringen?) 17 M 162 Niederjeutz (?) 21 M 162 Hagendingen 26 M 162 Machern.
163	St. Avold Adolf-Hitler-str. 30	WESTMARK		
164	Saarbrücken, Gutenbergstr. 49	WESTMARK		6 M 164 Saarbrücken 11 M 164 Saarlautern
165	Saarburg i. Lothr., Hermann-Göring-Str. 7	WESTMARK		16 M 165 Wich 24 M 165 Wich 27 M 165 Wich
181	Regensburg, 2, Dr-Martin-Lutherstr. 14	HUHNLEIN	SF ZELLER	3 M 181 Zwiesel 5 M 181 Straubing 11 M 181 Bodenwöhr 15 M 181 Zwiesel 21 M 181 Passau
187	Kempten i. Allau, Reichlinstr. 3	FRANKEN		2 M 187 3 M 187 Sonthofen 6 M 187 14 M 187 Memmingen 15 M 187 Eichstätt
188	Graz, Max-Reiner-Ring 5 III	Brig. STEIRMARK	SF KOHLHUBER	3 M 188 Graz-Stagersbach 23 M 188 Leibnitz 27 M 188 St. Martin 28 M 188 Deutschlandsberg ? M 188? Fürstenfeld

NO.	HQ. LOCATION	MOTORGRUPPE	COMMANDER	COMPONENT UNITS
189	Marburg a. Drau, Reiserstr. 1	Brig. STEIERMARK		
190		Brig. KÄRNTEN	OSF REUTHLINGER	4 M 190 Assling
191	Salzburg (possibly staffel)	Brig. SALZBURG		
192	Bregenz (possibly staffel)	Brig. TIROL VORARLBERG	SF. HANSLIK	? M 92 or 192 Feldkirch
193	Wien XX Jägerstr. 30	WIEN	HSF KRIST i.V.	I M 193 Wien XXI/141 II M 193 Wien III M 193 Wien IV M 193 Wien II/27 V M 193 Wien 2 M 193 Wien XXI/146 3 M 193 Wien XXII/147 11 M 193 Wien XXI/145 22 M 193 Wien XXI/141 25 M 193 Wien XXI/141 32 M 193 Wien II/27 33 M 193 Wien II/27 34 M 193 Wien II/27 41 M 193 Wien XX/20 43 M 193 Wien XX/20 45 M 193 Wien XX/20

NO.	HQ. LOCATION	MOTORGRUPPE	COMMANDER	COMPONENT UNITS	
194	Wien XII, Singrienerst. 19	WIEN		I M 194 Wien	
				II M 194 Wien	X/75
				III M 194 Wien	XII/82
				IV M 194 Wien	
				V M 194 Wien-Mödling,	XXV
				1 M 194 Wien	XI/79
				2 M 194 Wien	XI/79
				4 M 194 Wien-Gramatsneusiedl,	XXIII
				11 M 194 Wien	III/75
				12 M 194 Wien	X/75
				13 M 194 Wien	X/75
				14 M 194 Wien	X/75
				15 M 194 Wien	X/75
				16 M 194 Wien	X/75
				21 M 194 Wien	XII/82
				22 M 194 Wien	XII/82
				23 M 194 Wien	XII/87
				24 M 194 Wien	XII/87
				25 M 194 Wien	XIII/89
				31 M 194 Wien-Liesing,	XXIV
				32 M 194 Wien-Siebenhirten,	XXIV
				33 M 194 Wien-Perchtoldsdorf	XXIV
				34 M 194 Wien-Rodaun,	XXIV
				41 M 194 Wien-Brunn-Maria-Enzersdorf	XXV
				42 M 194 Wien-Mödling	
196	Lundenburg, Konrad-Henlein-Str. 30	NIEDER-DONAU	? HECKENSTELLER	1 M 196 Lundenburg	
				21 M 196	
				23 M 196 Laa a.d. Thaya	
197	Wiener Neustadt, Promenade 4	NIEDER-DONAU	SF EICHENSEDER	31 M 197 Neunkirchen	
				? M 197? Asparn an der Zaya	
199	Krummau a.d. Moldau, Adolf-Hitler-Platz 11	OBERDONAU		II M 199 Kienberg	
				24 M 199 Leonfelden	
				? M 199 Krummau	
				? M 199 Kaplitz	

NO.	HQ LOCATION	MOTORGRUPPE	COMMANDER	COMPONENT UNITS
200	Aussig	SUDETEN		
201	Troppau, Ignatz-Benesch-Gasse 4	SUDETEN		
202	Jägerndorf, Robert-Hohlbaum-Str. 12	SUDETEN		12 M 202 Freudenthal 21 M 202 Sternberg 42 M 202 Prag
203	Mähr. Schönberg, Fuhrmannsgasse 8	SUDETEN		III M 203 Freiwaldau 21 M 203 Freiwaldau 22 M 203 Freiwaldau
204	Zwittau, Bahnhofstr. 14	SUDETEN		
205	Trautenau, Jahnstr. 10	SUDETEN		13 M 205 Arnau
206	Reichenberg, Lerchenfeldgasse 13	SUDETEN		3 M 206 Reichenberg or Gablonz 4 M 206 Reichenberg or Gablonz 13 M 206 Gablonz 24 M 206 Kratzau

NO.	HQ LOCATION	MOTORGRUPPE	COMMANDER	COMPONENT UNITS
207	Böhm Leipa Mozartstr. 1580	SUDETEN		21 M 207 Tetschen
208	Aussig, Schutzenstr. 37	SUDETEN		I M 208 Karbitz II M 208 Aussig III M 208 Leitmeritz IV M 208 Dauba 1 M 208 Karbitz 2 M 208 Karbitz 3 M 208 Karbitz 11 M 208 Aussig 13 M 208 Aussig 14 M 208 Aussig 15 M 208 Aussig 21 M 208 26 M 208 Leitmeritz 31 M 208 Dauba 32 M 208 Dauba
209	Brüx, Teplitzerstr. 14	SUDETEN	SF RICHTER	1 M 209 Teplitz-Schönau 2 M 209 Teplitz-Schönau 3 M 209 Teplitz-Schönau 13 M 209 Komotau 14 M 209 Bilin 24 M 209 Bilin 26 M 209 Ober Leutensdorf
210	Kaaden, Hans-Knirsch-Str. 625	SUDETEN		II M 210 Saaz

61442-1

NO.	HQ LOCATION	MOTORGRUPPE	COMMANDER	COMPONENT UNITS
211	Karlsbad, Dr.-Strobelberger-Str., Haus Gea	SUDETEN	SF MOHR	3 M 211 Karlsbad 4 M 211 Karlsbad 8 M 211 Karlsbad 9 M 211 Fischern 11 M 211 Dallwitz 12 M 211 Aich 16 M 211 Schlackenmühl 24 M 211 Schlaggenwald 26 M 211 Theusing 28 M 211 Tepl 35 M 211 Bergstadt-Platten 36 M 211 St. Joachimsthal
212	Eger, Konrad-Henlein-Strasse	SUDETEN		22 M 212 Falkenau
213	Mies Kirchengasse 8	SUDETEN		4 M 213 Pilsen-Kosolup 15 M 213 Liehn 23 M 213 Ronsperg
214	Mähr.-Ostrau, Gronwaldgasse 5	SUDETEN	Franz PFEIFER	III M 214 Olmütz 1 M 214 Mähr.Ostrau 24 M 214 Prosnitz
215	Prag II., Wenzelsplatz 45	SUDETEN	HSF STRANSKY i.V. Staff. Dr. KALTSCHMIED	II M 215 Kladno III M 215 Königgrätz
233	Meissen, Hindenburgstr.26	SACHSEN	i.V. KILCH	12 M 233 Nossen 22 M 233 Pulsnitz 24 M 233 Königsbrück 32 M 233 Grödnitz

NO.	HQ LOCATION	MOTORGRUPPE	COMMANDER	COMPONENT UNITS
252	Koblenz a. Rhein, Steinstr. 23			I M 252 Bad Kreuznach 2 M 252 Bad Kreuznach 6 M 252 Kirn 15 M 252 Traben-Trarbach
296	Znaim, Strasse der SA. 2a	NIEDER DONAU	Ostaff. SCHNIDERICH	21 M 296 Hollabrunn 22 M 296 Ziersdorf
299 (Staffel)	Budweis, Deutsches Haus	OBER DONAU		
313		SUDETEN		22 M 313 Bischofteinitz
396	Brünn Schramm-ring 4	NIEDER-DONAU	Hstuf. WEISS	IV M 396 Iglau
	M Staffel "SAAR" (independent of a Standarte) Saarbrücken, Betzenstr. 3	WESTMARK (?)		

PART FOUR

NSKK MOTORBOAT UNITS

Note: In the following list, the assignment of component units is mainly based upon deduction rather than definite evidence, and should not therefore be taken as final.

NO. or NAME and HQ LOCATION	MOTORGRUPPE	COMMANDER	COMPONENT UNITS
(a) Mb Standarten			
1. Berlin W-35, Graf Spee-Str.6	BERLIN(?)		31 Sturmboot 1 Berlin (Assault Boat Coy.)
2. (?)			
3. "OSTMARK"(?)	WIEN(?)	SF ENGELMANN	2 Mb3 Linz 4 Mb3 Klagenfurt
4. Stuttgart (Also identified:- Mb Staffel "SUDWEST" Friedrichshafen, Friedrichsstr. 30)	SÜDWEST(?)	SF DILLENBERG	2 Mb 4 Friedrich- shafen 5 Mb 4 Radolfzell
5. (?)			4 Mb 5 Ingolstadt
"RHEIN" Düsseldorf Steinstr. 4/6	NIEDERRHEIN(?)		1 Mb ? Düsseldorf
(b) Mb Units not identified as part of a Standarte			
III "Rhein-Mosel" Koblenz, Steinstr.23	RHEIN-MOSEL(?)		11 Mb III Köln 12 Mb III Köln 13 Mb III Köln

Stürme

3 Mb? Leipzig
? Mb? Hamburg
? Mb? Rostock
? Mb? Gmunden
1 MbTV Bregenz

CONFIDENTIAL

SUPREME HEADQUARTERS
ALLIED EXPEDITIONARY FORCE
Office of Assistant Chief of Staff, G-2
Counter-Intelligence Sub-Division
Evaluation and Dissemination Section

SUPPLEMENT TO THE NSKK OF THE NSDAP, EDS/G/3

A German Document dated the 21st July, 1943, has come to hand too late to be incorporated into the NSKK-Order of Battle. This document gives the Order of Battle and Addresses of all motor and motorboat regiments, as well as all independent motor, motorboat and traffic control batallions existing at that time. It is felt that the reader of the NSKK would profit by reading this document in conjunction with the Annexe A Part III of the Basic Handbook of the NSKK as the latter gives all identified component units of the Standarten as well as the names of their C.O.s.

The Basic Handbook has a few Standarten that are not in the following list and it is probable that these units were formed after July, 1943. However, units contained in the supplementary list which are not included in the book should be considered as additional identifications.

3rd October, 1944.

CONFIDENTIAL

Motorstandarte.	Location.
M 1	Insterburg, Belowstr. 1
M 2	Allenstein, Treudankstr. 25
M 3	Elbing, Hindenburgstr.
M 4	Königsberg, Gebauhrstr. 16-17
M 5	Marienwerder, Hermann-Göring-Str. 6a
M 6	Danzig, Holzmarkt 24
M 7	Köslin, Friedrichstr. 20
M 8	Schneidemühl, Mühlenstr. 2
M 9	Stettin, Schulstr. 1
M 10	Stralsund, Wasserstr. 79
M 11	Schwerin i. M., Marstall, Gr. Moor
M 12	*Hamburg, Beneckestr. 43
M 13	*Altona a. Elbe, Flottbecker Chaussee 16
M 14	Kiel, Wolkerdamm, Schifferer-Haus
M 15	Itzehoe, Feldschmiede 98 III
M 16	Schleswig, Bellmannstr. 19
M 17	Gleiwitz (O.-S.), Augustenstr. 10
M 18	Schweidnitz, Burgstr. 19
M 19	Breslau 13, Strasse der SA. 61
M 21	Liegnitz, Gartenstr. 9
M 22	Landsberg a. Warthe, Küstriner Str. 109 I
M 23	Frankfurt a. Oder, Regierungsstr. 19
M 24	Senftenberg (N.-L.), Schlesische Str. 42
M 26	Eberswalde, Neue Schweizerstr. 26
M 27	Potsdam, Augustastr. 20
M 28	*Berlin SW 68, Zimmerstr. 54
M 29	*Berlin W 57, Potsdamer Str. 92
M 30	"Ernst vom Rath", Berlin-Schöneberg, Badensche Str. 56
M 31	*Berlin SW 61, Belle-Alliance-Str. 22
M 33	"Paul Lein", Dresden-A. 1, Zinsendorfstr. 4
M 34	Chemnitz, Further Trift 11
M 35	Leipzig C 1, Brüderstr. 26/28
M 36	Plauen i. Vogtl., Adolf-Hitler-Str. 56
M 37	Torgau a. Elbe, Mühlenstr. 5
M 38	Halle, Königstr. 58
M 39	Halberstadt, Mahndorfer Str. 20
M 40	Watenstedt-Salzgitter, Ortsteil Lebenstedt
M 41	Gera, Adolf-Hitler-Platz 4
M 42	Weimar, Watzdorfstr. 73
M 43	Rudolstadt, Katharinastr. 30, Schliessfach 162
M 44	Eisenach, Karlstr. 1
M 45	Nordhausen, Neustadtstr. 9
M 46	Hanau a. M., Mühltorweg 3
M 47	Kassel, Bahnhofstr. 2
M 48	Marburg, Frankfurter Str. 53
M 49	Frankfurt a. M., Kettenhofweg 55
M 50	Darmstadt, Alexanderweg 6
M 51	Ludwigshafen a. Rhein, Oberes Rheinufer 33
M 52	Neuwied a. Rh., Dierdorfer Str. 203
M 53	Karlsruhe, Kriegsstr. 29
M 54	Freiburg i. Br., Maria-Theresiastr. 2
M 55	Stuttgart-S, Filderstr. 45, Postschliessfach 370
M 56	Ulm a. D., Münsterplatz 30
M 57	Göttingen, Litzmannstr. 1a
M 58	Braunschweig, Leonhardplatz 11
M 59	Hildesheim, Hermann-Römer-Str. 3
M 60	Uelzen i. Hann., Adolf-Hitler-Str. 5
M 61	Hannover, Hohenzollernstr. 42
M 62	Bremen, Delbrückstr. 18
M 63	Oldenburg, Auguststr. 4
M 64	Osnabrück, Seminarstr. 32

CONFIDENTIAL

Motorstandarte.	Location.
M 65	Bielefeld, Hindenburgstr. 13
M 66	Münster i. Westf., Krummestr. 10
M 67	Dortmund, II. Kampstr. 3
M 68	Arnsberg i. Westf., Hermann-Göring-Str. 22
M 69	Bochum, Neustr. 22
M 70	Gelsenkirchen, Dietrich-Eckart-Str. 9
M 71	Köln a. Rh., Kaesenstr. 4
M 72	Wuppertal-Elberfeld, Strasse der SA. 117
M 73	Essen, Bismarckstr. 27
M 74	Duisburg, Düsseldorfer Str. 102
M 75	Düsseldorf, Frafenberger Allee 261
M 76	Aachen, Kaiserplatz 9
M 77	Bayreuth, Richard-Wagner-Str. 6
M 78	Ansbach, Adolf-Hitler-Platz 8
M 79	Schweinfurt, Adolf-Hitler-Str. 9
M 80	Landshut, Untere Schwimmschulstr. 1
M 81	Regensburg, Dr.-Martin-Luther-Str. 14/0
M 83	Nürnberg, Fürther Str. 10, I
M 84	Kolbemoor, Adolf-Hitler-Str. 3 1/3 (Rosenheim)
M 85	Weilheim (Obb.), Münchner Str. 30
M 86	München 2, Herzog-Wilhelm-Str. 13
M 87	Augsburg, Frauentorstr. 25/II Rg.
M 88	"Siegfried Schott" Graz, Girardigasse 1
M 89	"Johann Schnner", Leoben, Sauragasse 1/II
M 90	"Artur Seeber", Klagenfurt, Viktringerring 2
M 91	"Alfred Janke", Salzburg, Kaigasse 39/I
M 92	Innsbruck, Südtirolerplatz 4
M 93	*Wien 18, Währingergürtel 40
M 94	*Wien 110, 18. Bezirk, Hasenauer Str. 63
M 95	Coburg, ob. Bürglass 9
M 96	Krems, Heinemannstr. 5
M 97	Eisenstadt-Oberberg, 178, Postfach 83 (Eisenstadt)
M 98	St.Pölten, Nieder-Donau, Rossmarkt 1a
M 99	Linz a. Donau, Landstr. 36
M 100	Gmunden, Ob. Donau, Hochmüllergasse 11
M 101	Lötzen, Hindenburgstr. 1
M 102	Rastenburg, Ordensschloss
M 103	Tilsit, Hohe Str. 42 I
M 105	Thorn, Hermann-Göring-Str. 104
M 106	Bromberg, Weltzienplatz 1
M 107	Stolp i. P., Hindenburgstr. 44
M 108	Stargard, Heilige Geiststr. 19
M 111	Rostock i. Mecklb., Blucherplatz 1/L
M 112	Neuruppin, Fehrbelliner Str. 5
M 113	Lübeck, Werftstr. 2
M 114	Posen, Richard-Wagner-Str. 2
M 115	Hohensalza, Bahnhofstr. 21
M 116	Litzmannstadt, Adolf-Hitler-Str. 53
M 117	Oppeln i. Schles., Zimmerstr. 4
M 118	Görlitz, Bei der Peterskirche 12
M 119	Kattowitz, Ludendorff- Ecke Kalidestr., Bar. 23
M 120	Glogau, Langestr. 28
M 121	Anschrift wie bei M 119
M 122	Guben, Alte Poststr. 46
M 123	Krakau, 1, Weichselstr. 5, Postfach 1090
M 124	Lissa, Lindenstr. 42
M 125	Gnesen, Tremessener Str. 33
M 126	Kalisch, Hermann-Göring-Str. 17
M 133	Zittau i. Sa., Bahnhofstr. 15
M 135	Dessau, Ruststr. 1
M 136	Zwickau, Platz der SA. 6

CONFIDENTIAL

Motorstandarten.	Location.
M 137	Magdeburg, Göringstr. 18a
M 138	Weissenfels a. Sa. le, Zeitzer Str. 78 Haus der NSKK
M 141	Mittweida i. Sa., Max-Beulich-Str. 19
M 142	Erfurt Dalbergsweg 30
M 146	Aschaffenburg, Treibgasse 24
M 147	Giessen, Frankfurter Str. 33
M 148	Wiesbaden, Langsee 9
M 149	Luxemburg, Liebfrauenstr. 42
M 150	Mainz, Kaiserstr. 30
M 151	Kaiserslautern, Dr.-Martin-Luther-Str. 18
M 152	Trier, Thyrsusstr. 45
M 153	Heidelberg, Neue Schlossstr. 7
M 154	Hagenau i. Els., Strassburger Str. 3
M 155	Heilbronn a. N., Dittmarstr. 16
M 156	Konstanz a. B., Adolf-Hitler-Ufer 9
M 157	Strassburg, Neuweilerhofstaden 6
M 158	Colmar, Schlumberger Str. 11
M 159	Mühlhausen, Kanispfad 35
M 160	Lüneburg, Neue Sülze 6a
M 161	Diedenhofen, Berschulstr. 30
M 162	Metz, Bismarckstr. 12
M 163	St. Avold, Adolf-Hitler-Str. 30
M 164	Saarbrücken, Gutenbergstr. 49
M 165	Saarburg, i. Lothr., Hermann-Göring-Str. 7
M 181	Regensburg, 2, Dr.-Martin-Luther-Str. 14
M 187	Kempten i. Allgäu, Reichlinstr. 3
M 188	Graz, Max-Reiner-Ring 5 III
M 193	*Wien XX, Jägerstr. 30
M 189	Marburg a. Drau, Reiserstr. 1
M 194	*Wien XII, Singriener Str. 19
M 196	Lundenburg, Konrad-Henlein-Str. 30
M 197	Wiener Neustadt, Promenade 4
M 199	Kruman a. d. Moldau, Adolf-Hitler-Platz 11
M 201	Troppau, Ignatz-Benesch-Gasse 4
M 202	Jägerndorf, Robert-Kohlbaum-Str. 12
M 203	M.-Schönberg, Fuhrmannsgasse 8
M 204	Zwittau, Bahnhofstr. 14
M 205	Trautenau, Jahnstr. 10
M 206	Reichenberg, Lerchenfeldgasse 13
M 207	Böhm.-Leipa, Mozartstr. 1580
M 208	Aussig, Mozartstr. 1
M 209	Brüx, Teplitzer Str. 14
M 210	Kaaden, Hans-Knirsch-Str. 625
M 211	Karlsbad, Dr.-Strobelberger-Str. Haus Gea
M 212	Eger, Konrad-Henlein-Str.
M 213	Mies, Kirchengasse 8
M 214	Mährisch-Ostrau, Grönwaldgasse 5
M 215	Prag II, Wenzelsplatz 45
M 233	Meissen, Hindenburgstr. 26
M 252	Koblenz a. Rhein, Steinstr. 23
M 296	Znaim, Strasse der SA. 2a

CONFIDENTIAL

SM-STAFFEL.

M St 299	*Budweis, Deutsches Haus
M 396	Brünn, Schramring 4
M Saar	*Saarbrücken, Betzenstr. 3
Mb 1	*Berlin W 35, Graf Spee-Str. 6
Mb Rhein	*Düsseldorf, Stromstr. 4/6
Mb Ostmark	*Wien I, Hessgasse i/III/18

*S. Mb-Staff. Rhein-Mosel, Koblenz a. Rh., Steinstr. 23
*S. Mb-Staff. Südwest, Friedrichshafen, Friedrichstr. 30
*Verkehrsstaffel Gross-Hamburg, Hamburg 13, Johnsallee 67 I
*Verkehrsstaffel Berlin, Bln.-Charlottenburg, Knesebeckstr. 80/81
*Verkehrsstaffel Wien, Wien III, Metternichgasse 4

*These Units have no Road Aid
or Traffic Assistance Service.

CONFIDENTIAL

SUPREME HEADQUARTERS ALLIED EXPEDITIONARY FORCE
EVALUATION AND DISSEMINATION SECTION
G-2 (Counter Intelligence Sub-Division)

BASIC HANDBOOK

THE NSKK

(Das Nationalsozialistische Kraftfahrkorps)

NATIONAL SOCIALIST

MOTOR CORPS

AMENDMENT No. 3

ANNEXE B
NSKK GAZETTEER (Revised)

1. The attached Annexe B is revised to conform
   with the new information in Annexe A (Amdt. No.1
   of 8 Feb.45)

2. It should replace original Annexe B, pp.B1-B13.

3. This page should be retained as a coverpage.

E.D.S./G/3
Revised by EDS and
MIRS (London Branch)   13 March 1945

CONFIDENTIAL

ANNEXE B

NSKK GAZETTEER

(List of identified locations of NSKK Units and HQ'S)

LOCATION	UNIT(S)
Aachen	M 76
	I M 76
	II M 76
	1 M 76
	2 M 76
	3 M 76
	4 M 76
Adorf	III M 36
Ahrens	III M103
Aich	12 M211
Allenstein	M 2
Alsfeld	12 M147
Altdorf	12 M 83
Altena	13 M 68
Altenburg	III M141
	22 M141
Altona a Elbe	M 13
	1 M 13
	2 M 13
	3 M 13
Amberg	M 82
Anklam	4 M108
	14 M108
Annaberg-Buchholz	IV M 34
	21 M 34
	32 M 34
	33 M 34
	36 M 34
Ansbach	M 78
Antonienhütte	15 M119
Apolda	II M 42
	15 M 42
	18 M 42
Arnau	13 M205
Arnsberg i Westf.	M 68
Arnstadt ?	1 M 43
	2 M 43
Aschaffenburg	M146
	3 M146 ?
Aschersleben	14 M 52
Asparn an der Zaya	? M 97 ?
	? M197 ?
Assling	4 M190
Aue	12 M 36
Auerbach	32 M 36
Augsburg	M 87
	6 M 85
	(M. Br. Schwaben)
Auschwitz	14 M121

CONFIDENTIAL

CONFIDENTIAL

LOCATION	UNIT(S)
Aussig	M 200
	M 208
	II M 208
	11 M 208
	13 M 208
	14 M 208
	15 M 208
Ayrensbök	2 M 14
Azarlej	25 M 119
Bad Doberan	43 M 111
Bad Harzburg	21 M 59
Bad Homburg	12 M 49
Bad Kreuznach	I M 252
	2 M 252
Bad Lippspringe	14 M 65
Bad Mergentheim	I M 78
Bad Reicherhall	13 M 84
Bad Tennstedt	11 M 142
Bad Wildungen	22 M 48
	II K 48
Bad Zwischenahn	4 M 53
Baden	? M 97 ?
Baden-Baden	23 M 53 ?
Barmbeck	14 M 13
Barmstedt	2 M 113
Bärwalde	13 M 7
Bautzen	11 M 133
Bayreuth	M 77
Beckum	8 M 66
Belgarl	2 M 7
Bendsburg	9 M 119
Berga	5 M 63
Berge	5 M 64
Bergstadt-Platten	35 M 211
Berlin	M 25 ?
	M 28
	Ehrensturm Berlin
	M 29
	M 30
	M 31
	41 M 31
	M 32 ?
	42 M 32
	Mb 1
	31 Sturmboot 1
	(M.O Gr. Mitte-West)
	(M. Gr. Berlin)
Beuthen	II M 17
	1 M 17
	15 M 17
Biederitz (bei Magdeburg)	III M 137

CONFIDENTIAL

CONFIDENTIAL

LOCATION	UNIT(S)
Bielefeld	M 65
	I M 65
	1 M 65
	2 M 65
Bielitz	II M 121
	III M 121
Bielosowicz	16 M 119
Bilin	14 M 209
	24 M 209
Birkenwerder	I M 26
Bischheim	5 M 157
Bischofswerda	II M 133
Bischofteinitz	22 M 313
Bismarckhütte	12 M 119
Blankenburg (Leipzig)	24 M 39
Blankenburg (Nieder-Sachsen)	26 M 61
Bleicherode	5 M 45
Bobrownik	22 M 119
Bocholt	21 M 66
Bochum	M 69
	II M 69
	11 M 69
	12 M 69
	16 M 69
	17 M 69
Bockwitz	12 M 37
Bodenwöhr	11 M 161
Böhm Leipa	M 207
Bonn	11 M 71
	12 M 71
	15 M 71
Bottrop	34 M 66
	3 M 70
Brandenburg	IV M 27
	31 M 27
	32 M 27
	33 M 27
Braunau am.Inn.	99 M 100
Braunschweig	M 58
	1 M 58
	2 M 58
Bregenz	M 192
	1 Mb T.V.
Bremen	M 62
	15 M 62
	16 M 62
	(M Gr. Nordsee)
Breslau	M 19
	IV M 19
	31 M 19
	35 M 19
	37 M 19
	41 M 19
	43 M 19
	46 M 19
	(M.O.Gr.Ost)
	(M.Gr.Niederschlesien)
Brilon	6 M 68

CONFIDENTIAL

CONFIDENTIAL

LOCATION	UNIT(S)
Bromberg	M 106
	3 M 106
	M 130
Brunn (bei.Wien)	41 M 194
Brünn	M 396
Brüx	M 209
Bückeburg	18 M 61
Budweis	M 299
Bunzlau	21 M 21
Büren	12 M 65
Burgen	II M 150
Burgstadt	15 M 141
	21 M 141
Bützow	14 M 111
Cannstadt	4 M 55
Castrop-Rauxel	24 M 69
	25 M 69
Celle	III M 60
	21 M 60
Chemnitz	M 34
	1 M 34
	3 M 34
	4 M 34
	5 M 34
	6 M 34
	11 M 34
	12 M 34
	13 M 34
	14 M 34
	15 M 34
	52 M 34
Cloppenburg	25 M 63
Coburg	M 95
	14 M 77
Coesfeld	11 M 66
Cottbus	21 M 122
	24 M 122
Crailsheim	12 M 78
Crimmitschau	6 M 136
Cuxhaven	14 M 160
Dallwitz	11 M 211
Danzig	M 6
	5 M 6
	22 M 6
	23 M 6
	(M.O.Gr.Nordost)
	(M.Gr. Danzig-Wpr.)
Dargon	42 M 111
Darmstadt	M 50
Dassow	4 M 11

CONFIDENTIAL

LOCATION	UNIT(S)
Dauba	IV M 208
	31 M 208
	32 M 208
Daun	III M 152
Delitzsch	32 M 38
Delmenhorst	III M 63
	21 M 63
	26 M 63
Demmin	15 M 10
	16 M 10
Dessau	M 135
	III M 135
	1 M 135
	2 M 135
	3 M 135
	5 M 135
	(M Gr. Magdeburg-Anhalt)
Deutsch Krone	2 M 8
	4 M 8
Deutschlandsberg	28 M 188
Deutscho ? (in Lothringen)	12 M 162
Diedenhofen	M 161
	2 M 161
	7 M 161
	II M 162
Dietfurt	24 M 125
Dippoldiswalde	2? M 33
Donaueschingen	12 M 54
Donauwörth	16 M 87
Dortmund	M 67
	1 M 67
	2 M 67
	7 M 67
	33 M 67
	(M.Gr.Westfalen-Süd)
Dresden	M 33
	9 M 33
	12 M 33
	23 M 33
	41 M 33
	(M.Gr.Sachsen)
Duisburg	M 74
	3 M 74
Durlach	7 M 53
Düsseldorf	M 75
	I M 75
	8 M 75
	9 M 75
	1 Mb ?
	Mb Stand. "RHEIN"
	(M.Gr.Niederrhein)

LOCATION	UNIT(S)
Eberswalde	M 26
	23 M 26
Ebstorf	11 M 60
	31 M 60
Eckartsberge	22 M 42
Eckernförde	14 M 14
Eger	M 212
Ehrenfriedersdorf	34 M 34
Eichstätt	15 M 187
Eilenburg	31 M 38
Eisenach	M 44
Eisenstadt	M 97
Elbing	M 3
Eldena	14 M 11
Elmshorn	13 M 13
	15 M 13
Emmendingen	41 M 54
Erfurt	M 142
	II M 142
	III M 142
	1 M 142
	4 M 142
	5 M 142
	6 M 142
	22 M 142
	23 M 142
Erkner	33 M 26
Erlangen	39 M 83
Eschingen	IV M 55
	31 M 55
	32 M 55
Eschwege	31 M 47
Essen	M 73
Esslingen	IV M 44
Falkenau	22 M 212
Falkensee	24 M 112
Falkenstein	IV M 36
Fallersleben	34 M 60
Feldbach (Steiermark)	13 M 88
Feldbach (Württemberg)	35 M 55
Feldkirch	? M 92
	or 192
Feuerbach	5 M 55
Filder	III M 55
Fischern	9 M 211
Flatow	1 M 8
Flechtorf	5 M 58
Flensburg	11 M 16
	14 M 16
	15 M 16
Flöha	22 M 34
	III M 36

LOCATION	UNIT(S)
Frankenberg/Eder	II M 48
	III M 48
	11 M 48
	22 K 48
Frankenberg (Sachs.)	21 M 34
Frankenthal	22 M 51
Frankfurt a.Main	M 49
	2 M 49
	5 M 49
	7 M 49
	8 M 49
	11 M 49
	21 M 49
	22 M 49
	23 M 49
	24 M 49
	(M.Gr.Hessen)
Frankfurt a.Oder	M 23
	(M.Gr.Mark Brandenburg)
Freiberg	61 M 34
	62 M 34
Freiburg i.Br.	M 54
	1 M 54
	3 M 54
	9 M 54
Freiwaldau (Nieder Schlesien)	3 M 118
Freiwaldau (Sudeten)	III M 203
	21 M 203
	22 M 203
Freudenthal	12 M 202
Friedberg	III M 46
Friedenhorst	25 M 124
Friedenshütte	14 M 119
Friedland	13 M 102
Friedrichshafen	14 M 156
	2 Mb 4
Friedrichskoog	4 M 16
Friedrichsort	18 M 14
Fulda	11 M 46
	12 M 46
Fürstenfeld (Südwest)	? M 55
Fürstenfeld (Steiermark)	? M 88 ?
	? M 188 ?
Fürstenwalde/Spree	2 H 22
	13 M 23
	23 M 23
Fürth	32 M 83
	33 M 83
Gablonz	3 M 206 ?
	4 M 206 ?
	13 M 206
	(M.Gr.Sudeten)
Gaggenau	III M 53
Gänserndorf	? M 96 ?
Garmisch-Partenkirchen	II M 85
	2 M 85
Gebweiler	21 M 153

CONFIDENTIAL

LOCATION	UNIT(S)
Gelsenkirchen	M 70
	1 M 70
	2 M 70
	5 M 70
Georgswalde	26 M 133
Gera	M 41
Gersdorf	2 M 34
Gettorf	15 M 14
Gevelsburg	3 M 69
Giessen	M 147
	1 M 147
	4 M 147
Gladbeck	4 M 70
Glauchau	14 M 136
Gleiwitz (O.S.)	M 17
Glienicke	4 M 26
Glogau	M 120
	11 M 120
	12 M 120
Gmünden	M 100
	32 M 100
	? Mb ?
Gnesen	M 125
Göppingen	12 M 56
Görlitz	M 118
	11 M 118
	12 M 118
Goslar	III M 59
Gotenhafen	11 M 6
Gotha	1 M 44
Göttingen	M 57
Grabau	13 M 6
Grafenhainchen	III M 38
	21 M 38
Graz	M 88
	M 188
	I M 88
	II M 88
	1 M 88
	2 M 88
	3 M 88
	4 M 88
	5 M 88
	6 M 88
	7 M 88
	8 M 88
	11 M 88
	12 M 88
	13 M 88
	14 M 88
	15 M 88
	16 M 88
	17 M 88
	23 M 88
	3 M 188
	(M.Br.Steiermark)
Greifenberg	11 M 108
Greifswald	II M 10
Gremsmühlen	I 14
Greven	27 M 75
Grevesmühlen	6 M 11

CONFIDENTIAL

CONFIDENTIAL

LOCATION	UNIT(S)
Grödnitz	32 M 233
Gross Köllen	III M 2
Gross Linden	2 M 147
Grossschönau	29 M 133
Grünberg	14 M 147
Guben	M 122
Guhrau	1 M 120
Güstrow	13 M 111
	15 M 111
Gütersloh	3 M 65
Habelschwerdt	13 M 18
Hagenau im. Elsass	M 154
Hagendingen	21 M 162
Halberstadt	M 39
	1 M 39
	4 M 39
	6 M 39
Halle (Westf.)	4 M 65
Halle/Saale	M 38
	I M 38
	II M 38
	1 M 38
	2 M 38
	3 M 38
	4 M 38
	5 M 38
	6 M 38
	11 M 38
	12 M 38
	14 M 38
Hamburg	M 12
	12 M 12
	13 M 12
	21 M 12
	23 M 12
	24 M 12
	13 M 13
	? Mb ?
	(M.O.Gr. Nord)
	(M.Br. Hamburg)
Hameln	II M 61
	11 M 61
Hamm	12 M 67
	13 M 67
Hammerstein	12 M 107
Hanau a.M.	M 46
Hannover	M 61
	(M.Gr. Niedersachsen)
Hannover-Minden	15 M 47
	43 M 47
Hattingen	I M 69
Hecklingen	13 M 135
	35 M 137
Heidelberg	M 153
	12 M 153 ?
Heidenheim	IV M 56
Heidmühlen bei Neumünster	12 M 113
Heidrege	24 M 113

CONFIDENTIAL

LOCATION	UNIT(S)
Heilbronn a. Neckar	M 155
	4 M 155
	11 M 155
Helmstedt	24 M 58
Heppenheim	IV M 50
Herford	14 M 64
Herne	23 M 69
Herrenberg	23 M 55
Hersfeld	34 M 47
	I M 146
	1 M 146
	I K 146
	1 K 146
Heydekrug	6 M 103
	26 M 103
Hilden	7 M 72
Hildenhausen	11 M 44
Hildesheim	M 59
Hindenburg	14 M 17
Hirschberg	12 M 21
Hof	15 M 77
	35 M 77
Hohenlimburg	14 M 68
Hohensalza	M 115
Hohenstein-Ernstthal	15 M 136
Hollabrunn	21 M 296
Holzminden	IV M 59
Homburg/Saar	13 M 151
Horn	33 M 96
Hoya	22 M 62
Hoyerswerda	27 M 118
Husum	5 M 16
Idar-Oberstein	II M 152
	11 M 152
Iglau	IV M 396
Ingolstadt	4 Mb 5
Innsbruck	M 92
	I M 92
	II M 92
	5 M 92
	(M.Br.Tirol-Vorarlberg)
Insterburg	M 1
	M 103
	26 M 103
Itzehoe	M 15
	30 M 15
Jägerndorf	M 202
Jarotschin	42 M 124
Jenbach	24 M 92
Johann.Georgenstadt	15 M 36
Jungingen	22 M 156

CONFIDENTIAL

LOCATION	UNIT(S)
Kaaden	M 210
Kaiserslautern	1 M 151
	2 M 151
	31 M 151
	32 M 151
	(M.Gr.Westmark)
Kalisch	M 126
Kapfenberg	2 M 89
Kaplitz	? M 199
Karbitz	I M 208
	1 M 208
	2 M 208
	3 M 208
Karlsbad	M 211
	3 M 211
	4 M 211
	8 M 211
	(M.Gr.Sudeten, Egerland)
Karlsruhe	M 53
	I M 53
	3 M 53
Kassel	1 M 47
	2 M 47
	3 M 47
	4 M 47
	5 M 47
	6 M 47
	12 M 47
Kattowitz	M 119
	1 M 119
	2 M 119
	5 M 119
	M 121
	(M.Gr.Oberschlesien)
Kaysersberg	6 M 158
	15 M 158
Kempten i.Allgäu	M 187
Kevelaer	12 M 74
Kiel	M 14
	II M 14
	11 M 14
	12 M 14
	13 M 14
	16 M 14
	17 M 14
	18 M 14
	19 M 14
	18 M 15
	19 M 15
	(M.Gr.Schleswig-Holstein)
Kienberg	II M 199
Kirchdorf/Krems	14 M 100
Kirn	6 M 252
Kirschau	12 M 133
Kirschheim-Teck	7 M 103
Kitzbühel	22 M 92
Kladno	II M 215

CONFIDENTIAL

CONFIDENTIAL

LOCATION	UNIT(S)
Klagenfurt	M 90
	III M 90
	Mb 3
	(M.Br.KÄrnten)
Klingenthal	34 M 36
Klosterneuburg	43 M 94
Knittelfeld	11 M 88
Koblenz	M 252
	21 M 152
	MbIII
	(M.Gr.Rhein-Mosel)
Köflach	21 M 88
Kohlfurt	17 M 118
Kölleda	III M 45
Kolmar (Elsass)	M 158
Kolmar (Wartheland)	V M 114
Köln a. Rhein	M 71
	I M 71
	8 M 71
	11 MbIII
	12 MbIII
	13 MbIII
	(M.O.Gr.West)
Komotau	13 M 209
Königgrätz	III M 215
Königsberg	M 4
	31 M 4
	(M.Gr.Ostland)
Königsbrück	24 M 233
Königshofen	15 M 157
Königshütte	6 M 119
	11 M 119
Königstein	32 M 33
Konstanz a. Bodensee	M 156
Korbach	13 M 48
	III K 48
	21 K 48
Korneuburg	22 M 96
Köslin	M 7
	1 M 7
	2 M 7
	3 M 7
	4 M 7
Krainsburg	V M 90
Krakau	M 123
Kratzau	24 M 206
Krefeld	II M 75
Kremmen	22 M 112
Krems	M 96
Kreuzburg	11 M 117
Krotoschin	12 M 124
Krummau a.d.Moldau	M 199
	? M 199
Künzelsau	3 M 78
Küstrin	3 M 23
Kutno	IV M 115
Kyritz	5 M 112
	15 M 112

CONFIDENTIAL

LOCATION	UNIT(S)
Laa/Thaya	13 M 96
	23 M 196
Landsberg a.Warthe	M 22
	3 M 22
Landshut	M 80
Landstuhl	4 M 151
Langballig	12 M 16
Langen/Frankfurt a.M.	III M 49
Langenlois	34 M 96
Langensalza	13 M 27
	13 M 142
Langensalzen	13 M 47
Langführ	51 M 6
Lauban	15 M 118
	16 M 118
Lauffen	4 M 155
Laupheim	7 M 56
Laurahütte	6 M 119
Lauterbach	II M 147
Leer	18 M 63
	31 M 63
Lehnsalm	4 M 14
Leibnitz	23 M 188
Leipzig	M 35
	I M 35
	II M 35
	III M 35
	1 M 35
	2 M 35
	3 M 35
	4 M 35
	5 M 35
	6 M 35
	11 M 35
	12 M 35
	13 M 35
	14 M 35
	15 M 35
	21 M 35
	22 M 35
	24 M 35
	3 Mb ?
	(M.Gr.Leipzig)
Leitmeritz	III M 208
	25 M 208
Leoben	M 89
Leobschutz	23 M 117
Leonding-Paschitz	13 M 99
Leonfelden	24 M 199
Leslau	III M 115
	21 M 115
Lichtenstein (Sachs)	11 M 136
Liebnitz	44 M 111
Liegnitz	M 21
	1 M 21 ?
	4 M 21 ?
Liehn	15 M 213
Liepine	17 M 119
Liesen	? M 48 ?
Liesing	31 M 97
	33 M 97

CONFIDENTIAL

CONFIDENTIAL

LOCATION	UNIT(S)
Limbach	51 M 34
Lindau	15 M 85
Linderode	5 M 122
Linz a.Donau	M 99
	2 Mb 3
	(M.Gr.Oberdonau)
Lippstadt	23 M 67
Lissa	M 124
	1 M 124
Litzmannstadt	M 116
	1 M 116
	15 M 116
Loeben	26 M 119
Lörrach	32 M 54
Lötzen	M 101
Lübbecke	13 M 64
Lübeck	M 113
	I M 113
Luckenwalde	III M 27
Ludenscheid	12 M 68
Ludwigsburg	II M 55
Ludwigshafen a.Rhein	M 51
Ludwigslust	13 M 11
Lundenburg	M 196
	1 M 196
Lüneburg	M 160
	1 M 160
Luxemburg	M 149
Machern	26 M 162
Magdeburg	III M 39
	15 M 39
	21 M 39
	12 M 40
	7 M 135
	M 137
	2 M 137
	3 M 137
	4 M 137
	5 M 137
	6 M 137
	10 M 137
	12 M 137
	41 M 137
	42 M 137
	44 M 137
	51 M 137
	52 M 137
	53 M 137
	54 M 137
	55 M 137
	56 M 137
Mähr-Ostrau	M 214
	1 M 214
Mähr Schönberg	M 203
Mainz	M 150

CONFIDENTIAL

LOCATION	UNIT(S)
Malchow	16 M 11
	32 M 111
Malente	I M 14
Mannheim	I M 153
Marburg/Lahn	M 48
	I M 48
	1 M 48
	2 M 48
	3 M 48
	4 M 48
	I K 48
	1 K 48
Marburg. a.Drau	M 189
Maria-Enzersdorf	41 M 194
Marienberg	42 M 34
Marienhafen	12 M 63
Marienwerder	M 5
Markt Pongau	25 M 91
Marktredwitz	43 M 77
Marne	6 M 15
Mayrhofen	26 M 92
Meiningen	II M. 44
Meissen	M 233
Melle	3 M 64
Memel	? M 1 ?
Memmingen	14 M 187
Mendon	25 M 68
Metz	M 162
Mewe	26 M 5
Michelstadt	23 M 50
	23 M 146
Michendorf	5 M 27
Mies	M 213
Minden	II M 64
	11 M 64
Mittweida	M 141
	17 M 141
Mölin	5 M 113
Mollhagen	5 M 113
Moresnet	23 M 76
Morgenroth/Ruda	13 M 119
Moringen	15 M 57
Mühlhausen (Pr. Eylau)	15 M 3
Mühlhausen (Thur.)	2 M 45
Muhlheim	2 M 73
Mulhausen (Mulhouse)	M 159
München	M 86
	4 M 86
	5 M 86
	8 M 86
	10 M 86
	13 M 86
	17 M 86
	26 M 86
	(M.O.Gr.Süd)
	(M.Gr."Huhnlein")
München-Gladbach	III M 75
	21 M 75
	22 M 75

CONFIDENTIAL

LOCATION	UNIT(S)
Münster i.Westf.	M 66
	I M 66
	1 M 66
	2 M 66
	3 M 66
	4 M 66
	13 M 66
	(M.Gr.Westfalen-Nord)
Munster-Lager	6 M 160
Myslenice	8 M 119
Myslowitz	4 M 119
Nakle	24 M 119
Nauen	23 M 112
Naumburg	3 M 138
	4 M 138
	15 M 138
Neckarsulm	2 M 155
Neisse	4 M 117
Neubeckum	7 M 66
Neubrandenburg	22 M 111
Neudamm	1 M 22
	2 M 23
	11 M 23
Neudau	25 M 89
Neudorf	14 M 157
Neugersdorf	2 M 133
Neuharlingersiel	9 M 63
Neuhaus	15 M 160
Neumünster	13 M 15
Neunkirchen	31 M 197
Neunkirchen (Erzgeb.)	53 M 34
Neuruppin	M 112
Neustadt/Weinstrasse (Rhein)	12 M 51
Neustadt (Bdbg.)	3 M 112
Neustadt/O.S.	21 M 117
Niebüll	13 M 16
Niederjeutz (?)	1 M 161
	17 M 162
Niederwiesa	III M 36
Nienburg/Weser	21 M 62
Neuwied. a.Rhein	M 52
	II M 52
Nikolei	22 M 121
Nordhausen	M 45
	12 M 45
Northeim	14 M 57
Nortorf	II M 15
Nossen	12 M 233
Nürnberg	M 83
	(M.Gr.Franken)

CONFIDENTIAL

LOCATION	UNIT(S)
Oberhausen	11 M 73
Ober Leutensdorf	26 M 209
Oelsnitz	III M 36
	22 M 36
	23 M 36
Offenburg	32 M 53
	33 M 53
Ohrdorf	I M 44
Ohrdruf	5 M 44
Oldenburg	M 63
	1 M 63
	2 M 63
Olmütz	III M 214
Oppeln i. Schles.	M 117
Ortrand	IV M 37
Oschatz	3 M 141
Osnabrück	M 64
	I M 64
	1 M 64 ?
	6 M 64 ?
Osterode (Ostpr.)	23 M 2
Osterode (Sachs.)	12 M 57
Ottenstein	22 M 57
Pabianice	V M 116
Paderborn	II M 65
	11 M 65
Papenburg	24 M 64
Parchim	11 M 11
	1 M 112
Passau	21 M 181
Peine	II M 59
Perchtoldsdorf	32 M 97
Perg	2 M 99
Pforzheim	II M 53
Pilsen-Kosolup	4 M 213
Pinneberg	17 M 13
	25 M 113
Pirmasens	23 M 51
Pirna	21 M 33
	31 M 33
Plauen i Vogtland	M 36
Plock	? M 2
Plön	6 M 14
Posen	M 114
	2 M 114
	(M. Gr. Wartheland)
Possendorf	24 M 33
Pössneck	12 M 43
Potsdam	M 27
	1 M 27
	2 M 27
	3 M 27
Prag	M 215
	42 M 202
Prechlau	14 M 7

CONFIDENTIAL

LOCATION	UNIT(S)
Pr.Holland	14 M 3
	26 M 102
Pr.Mark	25 M 103
Prosnitz	24 M 214
Pulsnitz	22 M 233
Pyritz	4 M 108
Radolfzell	5 Mb 4
Rastatt	22 M 53
	23 M 53 ?
Rastenburg	M 102
Rathenow	4 M 112
	5 M 112
Redefin	4 M 11
Regensburg	M 81
	24 M 81
	M 181
	(M.Gr.Bayernwald)
Reichelsheim	III M 50
Reichenbach	4 M 36
	7 M 36
Reichenberg	M 206
	3 M 206 ?
	4 M 206 ?
Rendsburg	11 M 15
	13 M 15
	14 M 15
Retz	15 M 96
Reutlingen	46 M 55
	IV M 56
	31 M 56
	32 M 56
Reutte	14 M 92
Rheydt	III M 75
	23 M 75
	26 M 75
Ribnitz	4 M 111
Rinteln	12 M 61
Robel	15 M 11
	31 M 111
Rombach	III M 162
Ronsperg	23 M 213
Rosenberg	12 M 117
Rosenheim	M 84
Rostock i.Meckl.	M 111
	I M 111
	1 M 111
	2 M 111
	3 M 111
	4 M 111
	5 M 111
	53 M 111
	? Mb ?
	(M.Br.Hansa)

CONFIDENTIAL

CONFIDENTIAL

LOCATION	UNIT(S)
Rotenburg (Hessen)	2 K 146
Rothenburg	2 M 118
Rottweil	15 M 54
Rudolstadt	M 43
	11 M 43
Rumburg	25 M 133
Rümmingen	IV M 54
	31 M 54
Saarbrücken	M 164
	6 M 164
Saarburg i. Lothr.	M 165
Saarlautern	11 M 164
Saaz	II M 210
Sagau	4 M 118
Salzburg	M 91
	M 191
	(M.O.Gr.Alpenland)
	(M.Br. Salzburg)
Samter	31 M 114
Sangerhausen	24 M 45
Saulgau	32 M 156
Schieratz	22 M 116
Schivelbein	1 M 7
Schlackenmühl	16 M 211
Schladming	? M 89
Schlaggenwald	24 M 211
Schleswig	M 16
Schlönwitz	II M 8
Schneeberg	M 36
	11 M 36
Schneidemühl	M 8
Schöneck bei Magdeburg	IV M 137
Schonin	23 M 58
Schönlinde, Kr. Rumburg	24 M 133
Schönwalde	4 M 29
Schopfheim	33 M 54
Schoppinitz	3 M 119
Schötmar-Salzuflen	7 M 65
Schramberg	24 M 53
Schröttersberg	11 M 2
Schwabach	13 M 83
Schwanhof	26 M 77
Schwarzenberg	14 M 36
Schwaz	25 M 92
Schweidnitz	M 18
Schweinfurt	M 79
	1 M 79 (?)
Schwerin (Brandbg.)	11 M 22
Schwerin i.M.	M 11
	I M 11
	1 M 11
	2 M 11
	3 M 11
Schwerte	23 M 68
Seckenheim	21 M 153
Selbitz	IV M 77
Senftenberg (N-L)	M 24

CONFIDENTIAL

LOCATION	UNIT(S)
Sigmaringen	III M 156
Sinzheim	15 M 153
Soest	21 M 67
	22 M 67
Sonderhausen	14 M 45
Sonthofen	3 M 187
Sorau	3 M 122
Spandau	11 M 29
	12 M 29
	14 M 29
Sperlingshof	3 M 115
Speyer	11 M 51
Sprottau	1 M 118
St. Avold	M 163
St. Joachimsthal	36 M 211
St. Martin	27 M 188
St. Pölten	M 98
Stade	11 M 160
	12 M 160
Stadtilm	3 M 43
Stahlhammer O/S.	23 M 119
Stargard	M 108
Steinfurt	6 M 149
Sternberg	21 M 202
Stettin	M 9
	4 M 9
	11 M 9
	12 M 9
	13 M 9
	14 M 9
	15 M 9
	25 M 9 (M.b.Ostsee)
Steyr	I M 100
	3 M 100
Stockerau	2 M 96
Stolp i Pr.	M 107
Stopfersfurth	41 M 77
Stralsund	M 10
Strassburg	M 157
	2 M 157
	12 M 157
Straubing	5 M 181
Strelitz	13 M 117
Stuttgart	M 55
	I M 55
	1 M 55
	2 M 55
	3 M 55
	6 M 55
	7 M 55
	4 Mb.
	(M.O.Gr.Südwest)
	(M.Gr.Südwest)
Swinemünde	II M 108

CONFIDENTIAL

LOCATION	UNIT(S)
Tannheim	27 M 91
Tarnowitz	21 M 119
Telfs	13 M 92
Tepl	28 M 211
Teplitz-Schönau	1 M 209
	2 M 209
	3 M 209
Ternitz	62 M 97
Teschen	I M 121
	3 M 121
Tetschen	21 M 207
Themsing	26 M 211
Thorn	M 105
Tichau	27 M 121
Tilsit	M 103 ?
	M 104 ?
Torgau a. Elbe	M 37
Traben-Trarbach	15 M 252
Traunstein	12 M 84
Trautenau	M 205
Trebnitz	III M 19
Treia	3 M 16
Trempen	23 M 1
Treuen	33 M 36
Triberg	13 M 54
Trier	M 152
	1 M 152
	2 M 152
	3 M 152
Troppau	M 201
Trossingen	1 M 156
Tübingen	V M 55
	41 M 55
	42 M 55
	43 M 55
	47 M 55
	V M 56
	41 M 56
	43 M 56
	44 M 56
	47 M 56
Überlingen	3 M 156
Ueckermünde	IV M 9
	34 M 9
Ulm a. Donau	M 56
Ulzburg	12 M 13
Ülzen i Hannover	M 60
	II M 60
Unna	14 M 67

LOCATION	UNIT(S)	CONFIDENTIAL
Varel	8 M 63	
Vechta	I M 63	
	24 M 63	
Velbert	5 M 72	
Verden	17 M 62	
Viernen	14 M 74	
	14 M 75	
Villingen	11 M 54	
Vilseck	3 M 82	
Vilshofen	14 M 80	
Waizen-Kirchen	32 M 99	
Waldenburg	21 M 18	
Waldheim	13 M 141	
Wanne-Eickel	21 M 69	
	22 M 69	
Waren	17 M 11	
Warnsdorf	21 M 133	
	22 M 133	
	23 M 133	
Warthebrück	38 M 125	
Watenstedt-Salzgitter	M 40	
Weida	4 M 41	
Weiden	11 M 77	
Weikersheim	2 M 78	
Weilheim (Ober. Bayern)	M 85	
Weimar	M 42	
	24 M 142	
	(M. Gr. Thüringen)	
Weinheim	23 M 153	
Weissenfels	M 138	
	2 M 138	
Wels	? M 99 ?	
	? M 100 ?	
Welungen	15 M 126	
	23 M 126	
Wendlingen	34 M 56	
Werdau	5 M 136	
Werdohl	11 M 68	
Werfen	26 M 91	
Wernigerode	21 M 39	
Wesel	II M 74	
Wesermünde	1 M 62	
	2 M 62	
Wich	16 M 165	
	24 M 165	
	27 M 165	
Wien	M 93	
	M 94	
	M 193	
	M 194	
	I M 93	
	II M 93	
	III M 93	
	IV M 93	
	V M 93	
	1 M 93	
	2 M 93	
	3 M 93	

LOCATION	UNIT(S)
Wien (Cont'd.)	4 M 93
	5 M 93
	6 M 93
	7 M 93
	11 M 93
	14 M 93
	15 M 93
	16 M 93
	17 M 93
	21 M 93
	22 M 93
	23 M 93
	24 M 93
	25 M 93
	26 M 93
	31 M 93
	32 M 93
	33 M 93
	34 M 93
	35 M 93
	36 M 93
	37 M 93
	I M 94
	II M 94
	IV M 94
	V M 94
	1 M 94
	2 M 94
	3 M 94
	4 M 94
	5 M 94
	11 M 94
	12 M 94
	13 M 94
	21 M 94
	23 M 94
	24 M 94
	31 M 94
	32 M 94
	33 M 94
	34 M 94
	42 M 94
	43 M 94
	I M 193
	II M 193
	III M 193
	IV M 193
	V M 193
	2 M 193
	3 M 193
	11 M 193
	22 M 193
	25 M 193
	32 M 193
	33 M 193
	34 M 193
	41 M 193
	43 M 193
	45 M 193

CONFIDENTIAL

LOCATION	UNIT(S)
Wien (Cont'd.)	I M 194
	II M 194
	III M 194
	IV M 194
	V M 194
	1 M 194
	2 M 194
	4 M 194
	11 M 194
	12 M 194
	13 M 194
	14 M 194
	15 M 194
	16 M 194
	21 M 194
	22 M 194
	23 M 194
	24 M 194
	25 M 194
	31 M 194
	32 M 194
	33 M 194
	34 M 194
	41 M 194
	42 M 194
	Mb 3
	(M.O.Gr.Südost)
	(M.Gr.Niederdonau)
	(M.Gr.Wien)
Wiener Neustadt	M 197
Wiesbaden	M 148
Wilhelmshafen	7 M 63
	17 M 63
Wilster	III M 15
Wismar	3 M 11
	5 M 11
Wittenberg	I M 37
Wittenberge	12 M 112
Witter	18 M 69
Wittmund	13 M 63
Wittstock	25 M 137
Wollin	12 M 108
Wörgl	III M 92
Worms	III M 150
Wroschen	V M 124
Wunsiedl	V M 77
Wuppertal-Elberfeld	M 72
	3 M 72
Würzburg	II M 79
	32 M 155
Wurzen	I M 141
	2 M 141

CONFIDENTIAL

LOCATION	UNIT(S)
Zehdenick	11 M 26
Zell Am See	23 M 91
Zella-Mehlis	21 M 43
	3 M 44
	8 M 44
Zielenzig	III M 23
	21 M 23
Ziersdorf	22 M 296
Zinten	I M 3
Zittau i. Sachs.	M 133
	1 M 133
Znaim	M 296
Zoppot	I M 6
Zschopau	24 M 34
Zschorlau	13 M 36
Züllichen	I M 122
Zwettel	45 M 96
Zwickau	1 M 36
	2 M 36
	3 M 36
	8 M 36
	9 M 36
	10 M 36
	M 136
	4 M 136
Zwiesel	3 M 181
	15 M 181
Zwittau	M 204

CONFIDENTIAL

SUPREME HEADQUARTERS ALLIED EXPEDITIONARY FORCE
EVALUATION AND DISSEMINATION SECTION
G-2 (COUNTER INTELLIGENCE SUB-DIVISION)

BASIC HANDBOOK OF THE NSKK

ANNEXE C

Diagrams and Plates

E.D.S./G/3
Compiled by MIRS (LONDON Branch)
From Material Available at
WASHINGTON and LONDON

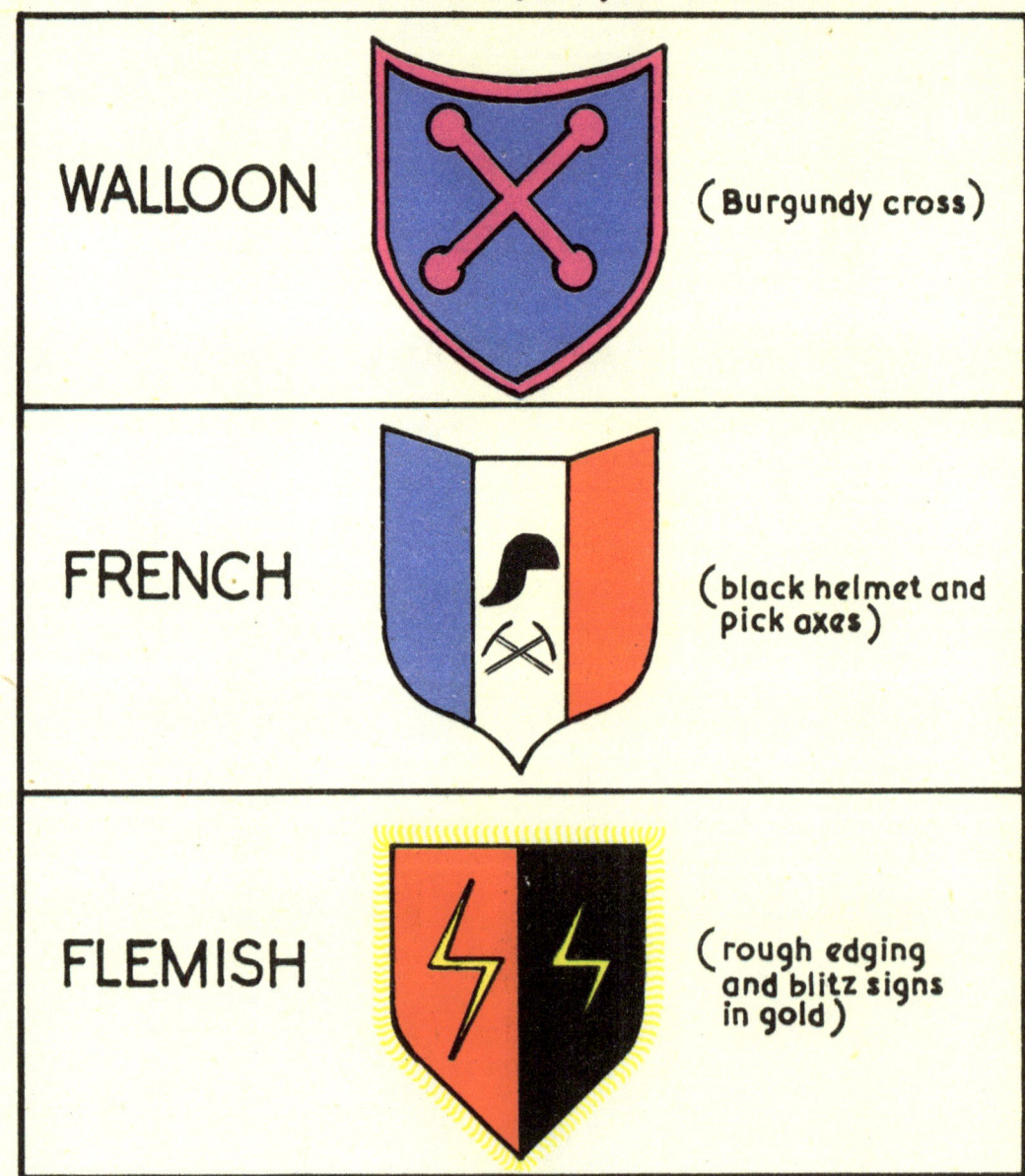

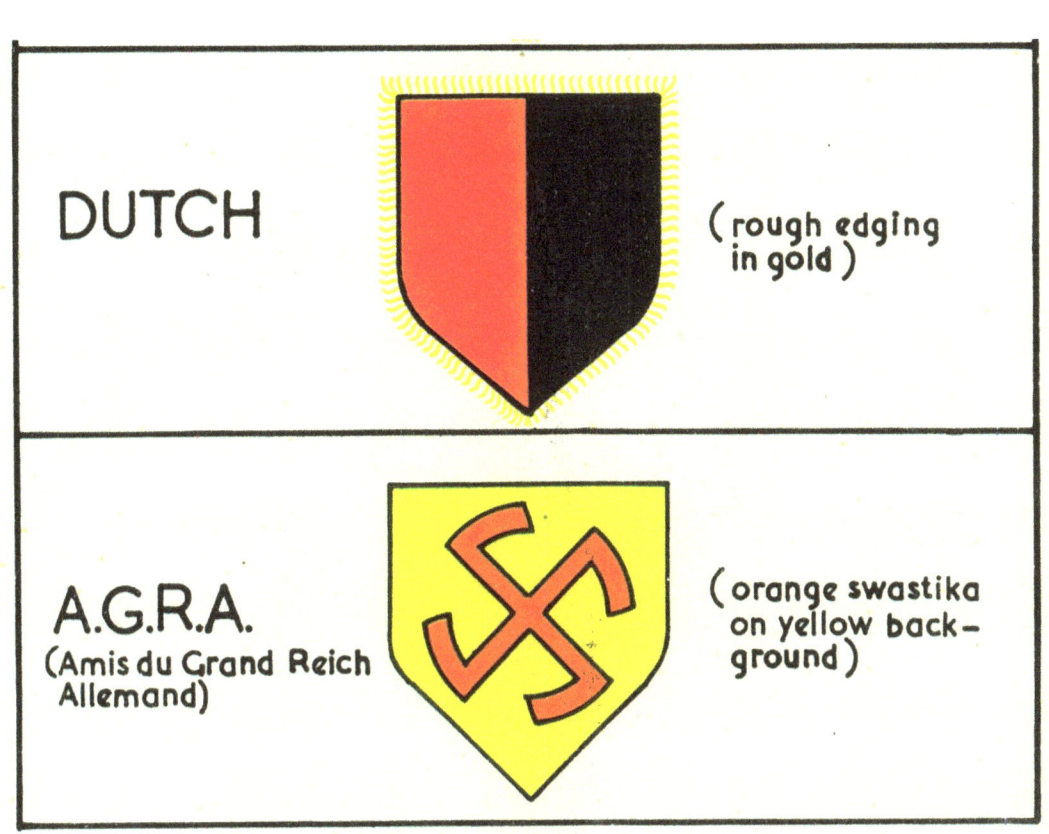

Escutcheons worn by non German NSKK personnel

Uniformen des NSKK.

Oberscharführer im M.-Sturm 2/M 86
im Überanzug

Uniformen der Kraftbootstandarte des NSKK.

Sturmführer
im Stab der Kraftbootstandarte 1
im großen Dienstanzug

Rottenführer
im Stab der Kraftbootstandarte 1
im Mantel

Achselstücke

NSKK.-Mann bis Obertruppführer
Motorgruppe Sachsen

Sturmführer bis Sturmhauptführer

Staffelführer bis Standartenführer

Oberführer

Brigadeführer bis Obergruppenführer

Korpsführer

Dienstmützen

NSKK.-Mann bis einschl. Obertruppführer
Motorgruppe Hochland

Feldmütze

Sturmführer im Stabe der Korpsführung

Sanitätsabzeichen

Ärzte

Sanitäts-Unterführer

Zahnärzte und Dentisten

Apotheker

Dienstgradabzeichen des NSKK.

NSKK.-Mann Sturm 11 der Motorstandarte 29

Sturmmann Sturm 1 der Motorstandarte 10

Rottenführer Sturm 19 der Motorstandarte 53

Scharführer im Stab der Korpsführung

Oberscharführer im Stab der Motorobergruppe Ost

Truppführer im Stab der Motorgruppe Kurpfalz-Saar

Obertruppführer im Motorsturm 16/M 80

Sturmführer des Motorsturms 9/M 86

Obersturmführer Führer des Lehrsturmes der Motorgruppe Hochland

Sturmhauptführer im Stab der Motorstandarte 51

Staffelführer Führer der Standarte 65

Oberstaffelführer Führer der Staffel III der Motorstandarte 86

Standartenführer Führer der Motorstandarte 85 oder im Stab

Oberführer im Stab der Motorgruppe Franken

Brigadeführer Führer der Motorgruppe Ostsee oder im Stab

Gruppenführer Führer der Motorbrigade Hochland

Obergruppenführer im Stab der Korpsführung

Korpsführer

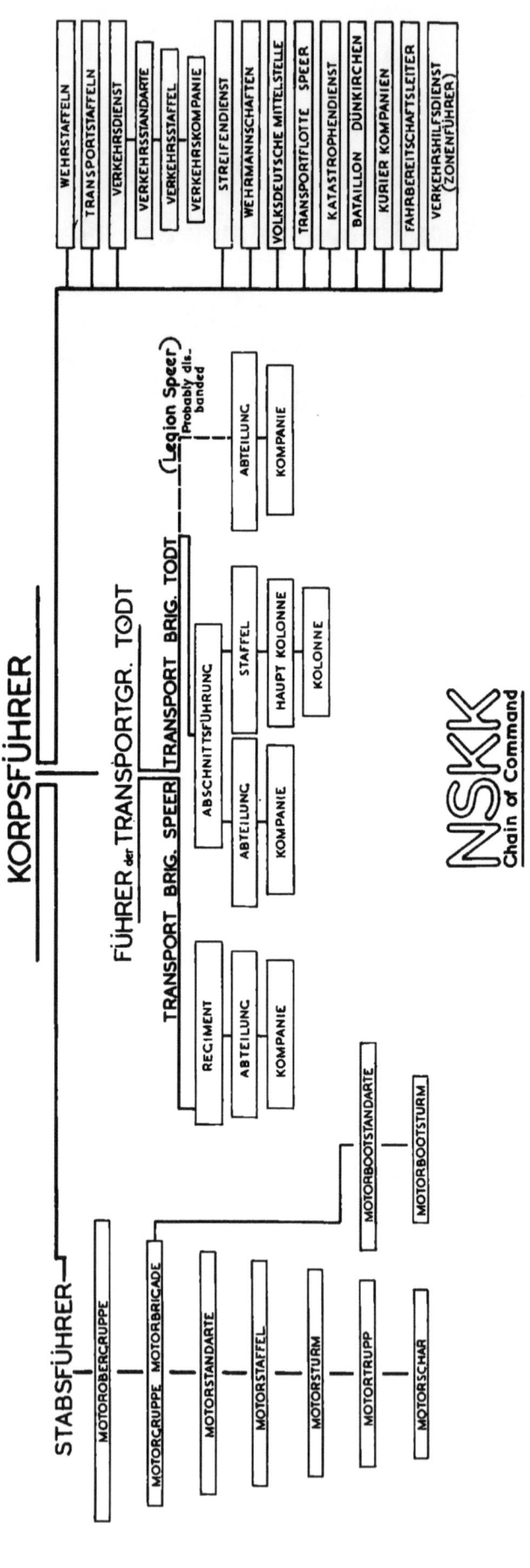

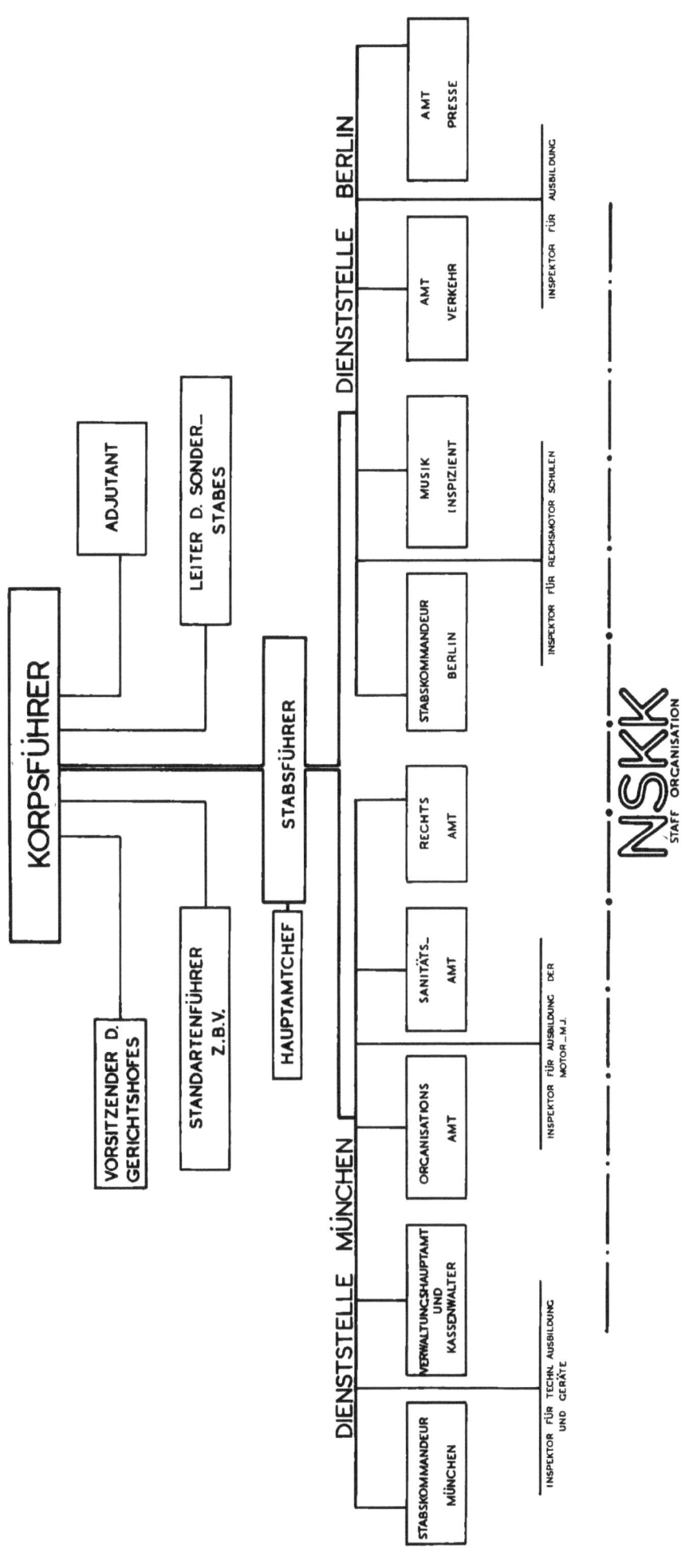

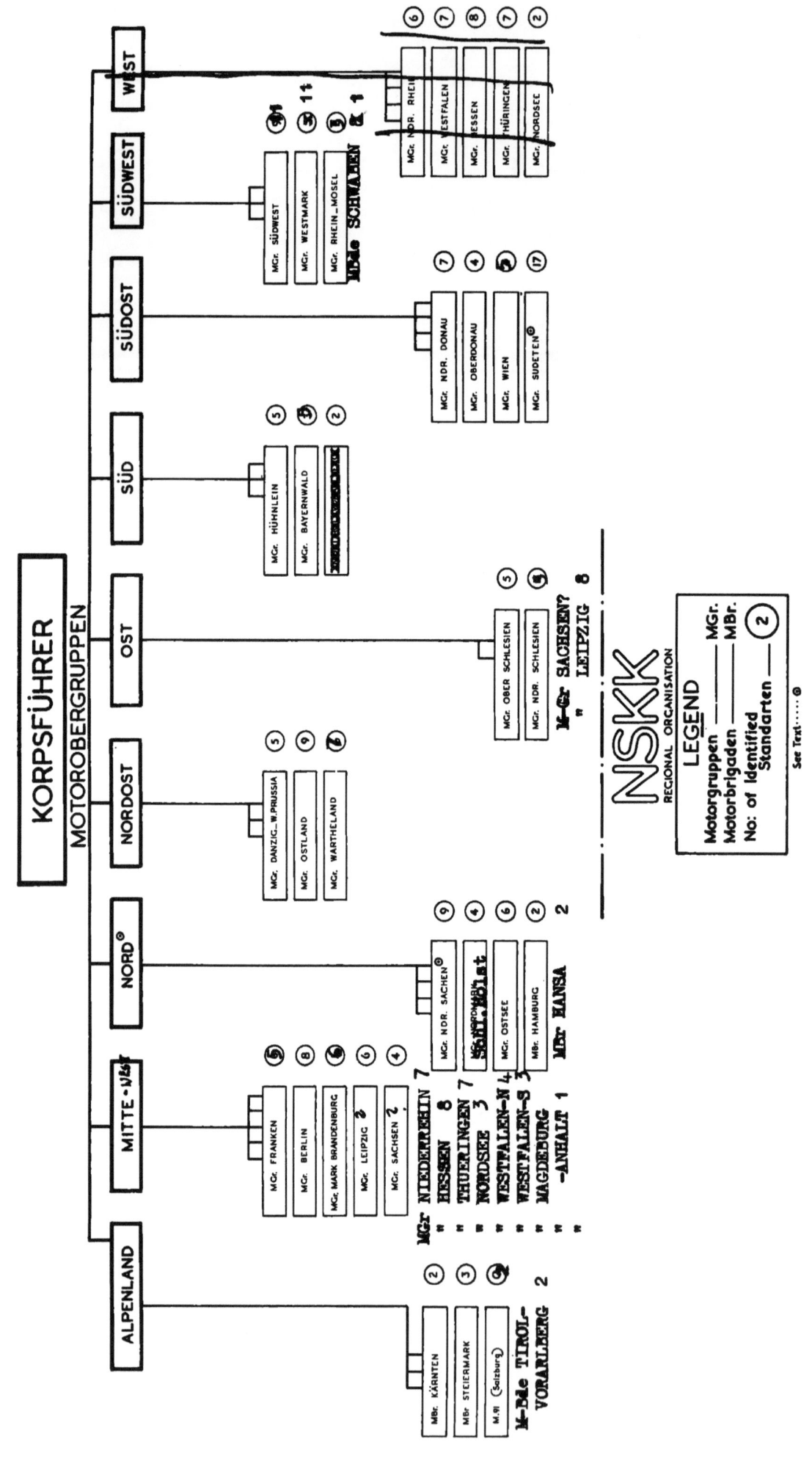

ANNEXE D.

ABBREVIATIONS LIKELY TO BE FOUND IN NSKK DOCUMENTS

A.G.R.A.	Amis du Grand Reich Allemand (Friends of the Great German Reich)
B	Motorgruppe Berlin
BF.	Brigadeführer
Br	Motorgruppe Mark Brandenburg
Eg	Motorgruppe Sudeten
Fr	Motorgruppe Franken
He	Motorgruppe Hessen
Hstuf. or HSF	Hauptsturmführer
Ho	Motorgruppe Hühnlein
i.V.	in Vertretung
Kfz.	Kraftfahrzeug
Kr.	Kreis
L	Motorgruppe Leipzig
Lkw.(LKW.)	Lastkraftwagen
M	Motor, Motorstandarte
Mb	Motorboot, Motorbootstandarte
M.Br.	Motorbrigade
M.Gr.	Motorgruppe
Motor-Hj.	Motor-Hitlerjugend
M.O.Gr.	Motorobergruppe
Ndr-	Nieder-
Nm	Motorgruppe Nordmark
No	Motorgruppe Nordsee
Nrh	Motorgruppe Niederrhein
Ns	Motorgruppe Niedersachsen
N.S.D.A.P.	Nationalsozialistische Arbeiter-Partei
N.S.K.K.	Nationalsozialistisches Kraftfahr-Korps
O.F.	Oberführer
OGF.	Obergruppenführer
ONS.	Oberste Nationale Sportbehörde für die Kraftfahrt
Os	Motorgruppe Ostsee
Ost	Motorgruppe Ostland
Ostaff. or OSF	Oberstaffelführer
Ostuf.	Obersturmführer
O.T.	Organisation Todt
S.A.	Sturm-Abteilung
Sa	Motorgruppe Sachsen
SF	Standartenführer
SS	Schutz-Staffel
Stabsfü.	Stabsführer
Staff.	Staffelführer
Stuf.	Sturmführer
Th	Motorgruppe Thüringen
Wf	Motorgruppe Westfalen
Wm	Motorgruppe Westmark
z.b.V.	zur besonderen Verfügung

INDEX OF SUBJECTS.

(NOTE: Subjects which can easily be found by reference to the Table of Contents have in most cases not been included in this Index.)

        Paragraph

Aachen	43.
Abbreviations, Unit	49.
Abbreviations, M. Gruppen	49.
Abwehr Abteilung	77.
Achern, Baden	43.
Afrika Korps	55
Alpenland, Motor Obergruppe	34, 50.
Ambulances	82
Amt. Presse	42
Amt. Verkehr	42
Armlets	50
Armament and War Production, Reich Minister	58.
Archiv, Presse und Kriegsgeschichte Abteilung	77
Archives, Press relations and Historical Section	77
Atlantic Wall	51
Bad Gandersheim (Harz)	43
Balkans	54
Baustab SPEER	52
Bayreuth – Saas	43
BB Schein	14
Beauftrager für den Motorisierten Transport der Kriegswirtschaft	4.
Beifahrer	63
Belgium	63
Berlin, Verkehrsstaffeln	13
BERND ROSEMEYER, Berlin (Training Unit)	12
Beschaffung OKH – Luft	76
Bessarabia (Volksdeutsche)	12.
Betriebsberechtigungsschein	14
Beurlaubtenstandes, Soldaten des	7.
BEYER-EHRENBURG, OGF	59.
BLANCK, Ostuf	76
BRÜCKNER, O. OF	63
BRÜNN, Motor Standarte 396	36
Buildings and Construction	80
Buttons	48, 49.
Cargo Inspection Service	16
Carniola	22
Cavalry Regiment SA	2
Charlottenburg – Berlin 9, (offices)	81
Chief of Staff of Party Propaganda Office	3
Chief of the German Staff	8
Constance, Lake	8
Counter Intelligence and Espionage	77
Courier Service	53
Court Martial	62
Criminal Police, Regional Command HQ's	15
Croatian Volunteers	63.

	Paragraph
Danube	16, 18
Danzig, Motor Standarte 6	36
Danzig, SA Brigade 6	36
Defence Badge	7.
DENK, Obergruppenführer Ritter Adolf von	40
Dental Clinics, Mobile	82
"Deutsche Kraftfahrt"	32
DIEDRICH, Oberstaffelführer	20
Dienstzeitbescheinungen	78
Diez/Lahn	43
Disciplinary Tribunal	79
Disziplinärgericht Abteilung	79
Döberitz (Motor School)	52
Döberitz, NSKK Bataillon	27
Döberitz, -Elsgrund	43
Donau-Flotille	21
DORIOT	63
Dramburg, Pommern	43
Drammen, Norway	44
Dresden, Motor Standarte 33	36
Drevis School	44
Driving Licences	5, 7.
Dutch Army	21
Dutch volunteers	63
Dünkirchen, Bataillon	27
Ebersbach, Motor Standarte 133	36
Economics and Administration	30, 80
Einsatzgruppe Südost	54
Einsatzüberwachung	75
EIX, Ostaff	42
Elbing, Motor Standarte 3	36
Emblems	71
Emergency Action Battalions	29
Emergency Service	33
Emsland, SA Pionier-Standarte	25
Epaulettes	48
EPP, Free Corps	4
EPP, Gen. Ritter von EPP Schule	43
EPP, 7th Reichwehr Division	4
Ersatzabteilung	61, 78
Escutcheons	64
Espionage and Counter Intelligence	77.
Fahrbereitschaftsleiter	9, 16
Feuer-Einsatz-Kommando der SA	29
Financial Control Section	74
Foreigners in NSKK	62, 63, 78
France	20, 57, 59, 63.
Frankfurt/Oder	43
FREISLER, NSKK Brigadeführer Dr. Roland	3
Führerschulen	47, 48.

	Paragraph.
Gebirgsmotorschule	43
GEITZ, Stürmfuhrer	74
Gericht und Rechtwesen	79
Gerichtshof	62
German Alpine Troops	53
GÖRING	4, 52.
Government Councillor	58
GREULICH, Ostaff	78
Groez, Thuringen	43
GROSSER, Ostuf	4
Grünberg, Schloss	29
GUDERIAN, Col. Gen	8
GRÜTKE, OGF	81
HADAMOVSKY, Gruppenführer Eugen	3
HAEFKE, Staffelführer	59
Hamburg, Motor Brigade	25
Hamburg, Verkehrsstaffeln	13
HASSE, Kriegsrangführer	76
Hasslinghausen	43
Hauptabteilungen der O.T.	74, 80
Haus-Revision	74
Heer, Transport Brigade	57
Heer, Transport Standarte	59
Heerstrasse, Berlin	61
HEIDEL, Staffelführer	74
HEISE, Dr. Staffelführer	62, 79
HELLMANCYK, Oberstaffelführer	25
Helsa bei Kassel	43
Hessen, Motorgruppe	3, 17
HESSEN, Obergruppenführer Richard Prinz von	3, 40
High Command of the Ground Forces	7
Highway Patrol Service	15
HITLER	3.
HITLER JUGEND	Foreword
Hochland, Motorgruppe	4
HOHENLOHE, Standartenführer z.b.V. August Prinz zu	3, 40
Holthausen bei Milspe	43
Home Defence Companies	22
HÜHNLEIN, Adolf	3,4,6,40.
HÜHNLEIN, Adolf Schule	43
HÜHNLEIN, Motorgruppe	50
Hülsen/Aller	43

	Paragraph
ILLIG, Ostaff	75
Ilmen, Lake	59
Immediate Rescue	29
Insignia	46,48,50,70.
Inspector of Automobile Schools	42
Inspector of Bands	42
Inspector of Mobile Troops	8
Inspector of Technical Training & Equipment	41
Inspector of Training	42
Inspector of Training of the Motor Hitler Youth	41
Inspektor der Reichsmotorschulen	42
Inspektor für Ausbildung	42
Inspektor für Ausbildung der Motor-Hitler Jugend	41
Inspektor für Technische Ausbildung und Geräte	41
Italien, Abschnittsführung	60
Italy	59
Itzehoe	43
JÄGER, Adolf	40
Judicial and Legal Matters	79
JÜRGENSEN, Obergruppenführer	6
Katastrophen Einsatz Staffel	29
Katastrophendienst	29, 33
Kaukasien, Abschnittsführung	60
KEITEL, Gen. F.M. KEITEL Schule	43
KIESSLING, Staffelführer	59
KOBLITZ, Staffelführer	59
Klagenfurt, Motor Standarte 90	36
Kommando Volksdeutsche Mittelstelle	23
KÖBELE, GF August	41
Kochel am See	43
Kraftwagen Transport Abteilung	60
Kraftfahrzeug, Lager und Ausrustung	76
Krakau, Kurierkompagnie	20
KRAUS, Obergruppenführer Erwin	4,41,58
Kreiensen (Harz)	43
KREUZLIN, GF Hans	42
Kriegskraftfahrschein	7
"Kriegspost"	32
Kriminalpolizeileitstellen	15
KUNZ, Staffelführer	59

	Paragraph
LAGRANGE, Staff	81
Landsberg Prison, Bavaria	4
LANGHAMMER, Ostuf	75
Legal and Judicial Affairs	41, 79
Legion SPEER	61, 62, 66
Leipzig-Rochlitz	43
Leistungsabzeichen, Motor HJ	6
Lemberg, Verkehrskompagnie	13
Limburg, Belgium	44, 63
Linz	16
LKW Staffeln	51
LORENZ, Obergruppenführer	23
Lorry Battalions	51
Lower Styria	22
Loyalty Badge	50
Luft, Motorgruppe	57, 59
Luft, Transport Brigade	57
Luftwaffe	Forward 5, 57, 59, 68, 73, 76.
Lundenburg, Motor Standarde 196	36
Lyck, Ost Preussen	43
MANDT, Ostuf	75
Marine SA	38
MARSCHALIK, Herr	78
MARTIN, BF Jost	42
Medical Section	81
Medical Department	41
Militärstrafgesetzbuch	62
Military Defence Training Department	42
Military Penal Code	62
Mittweida	43
Mobile Dental Clinics	82
Mobilisation	78
Mobstelle	78
Motorboat units	8; 18, 21, 33.
Motorbootstürme	18, 21, 33
Motor Gruppe Luft	57, 59
Motor HJ	Foreword 4, 6, 8, 38
Motor Schools	43.
Motorsport Schulen	6, 7
Motor Sport Schools	6, 7
Motor Sport, Supreme Nat. Authority for	4, 45
Motorstürme der SA	1, 2, 3.
Motorised Home Guard	7.
Motorised Medical Battalions	82
Moorweide, Transport Staffel	25
Muhlberg	43
München	42, 43.
München-Gladbach-Rheindahlen	43
Munich	4
Musikinspizient	42.

	Paragraph
NAGEL, Gruppenführer Willy	24, 58, 69, 74
National Officers Academy of the NSKK	43
National Tyre Depot	30
Nederland, Motorschule	63, 44
Nederland, Regiment	39, 59, 63.
NEY, Ostaff, Bruno	41
Niedersachsen, Motor Gruppe	34
NORD, GF, E.J.	40
Norway	53
Norwegen, Abschnittsführung	60
NS Automobil Klub	3
NSFK	Foreword
"NSKK-Mann, der"	32
Oberschlesien, Motor Gruppe	20, 48, 49
Oberste Nationale Sportbehörde für die deutsche Kraftfahrt	4, 45.
Offices of the Supreme Command – Berlin	42
Offices of the Supreme Command – Munich	41
Official Gazette on Traffic Regulations	14
"ONS-Mitteilungen"	32
Ordnance	76
Organisationsamt	41
Organising H.Q.	20
Ostland, Motor Gruppe	48, 49
OTTOWEILER	43.
Panzer	53
Panzertruppen	6, 7.
Parteigericht	62
Party Propaganda Office, Chief of Staff	3
People's Court, President of	3
Poland	20, 53
Police Forces	5, 9
Police Patrol Service	75
Polizei Kompanien	20
Polizei Regimenter	20
Polizeiverkehrskompagnie	13
Posen, Verkehrskompagnie	13
Producer Gas Motors	5
Quartiermeister Dept.	76
Quartermaster Dept	76

	Paragraph
Racial Germans	63
RASTENBURG (SA-Brigade 3)	36
Rechtsamt	41
Rechtshilfe und Klagesachen	79
Rechtwesen und Gericht	79
Regensburg	43
Reich Defence Commissioners	29
Reich Defence District	33
Reich Schools	43,47,49
Reichsführerschule	43,47,49
Reichsmotorsportschule	43
Reichsreifenlager	30
Reichstelle Asbest und Kautschuck	30
"Reichverkehrsblatt"	14
Reichsverteidigungskommissäre	29
Reichsverteidigungsgau	33
Reichswehr, Division, EPF's 7th	4
Reichswehrministerium	8
Reiterstandarten SA	2
Replacement Btn.	61
Reservists	7
REUSNER, Oberstaffelführer	74,76,78
Rhein-Flotille	21
Rhine	18, 21.
RIEDMAIER, GF Dr. A.	41
Road Aid Service	33
Road Air or Traffic Assistance Service	17
Road Zone Controller	17
Röhm	4.
Rommel	55
Rubber and Asbestos Control Authority	30
Ruhrland	43
RULAND, BF Theodor	41
Russia	56,59,63
Russland, Einsatzgruppe	63.

S.A.
S.A. Brigade	2
S.A. Gruppenführer	2
S.A. Pionier - Standarte EMSLAND	25
S.A. Reiterstandarten	2
S.A. Wehrabzeichen	7.
S.A. Wehrmannschaften	7, 22.
SALOMON, Pfeffer von (Capt)	3, 4.
SAMSE, Verwaltungsführer	80
Sanitätsamt	41
Sanitätskraftfahrzeug Staffel	82
Schiffsführerschule	8, 43
SCHIRACH, Baldur von	6
Schloss Grünberg, Sudetenland	29, 43
Schloss Hof, Sachsen	43
School for boat-mates	8, 43
SCHOTTEN, Ostuf	75
Schweidnitz-Kroischwitz, Schlesien	43
Schweina, Thüringen	43
Schwerin	43
SEIDEL, Josef	40
SIKORSKI, Dr. Stuf	81
Soforthilfe	29

	Paragraph
SPECHT, Major	78
SPEER, Prof. Albert	52, 58
SPEER Baustab	68
SPEER, MT Brigade	53,58,59 61, 63
SPEER, MT Standarte	52,53,55
SPEER, Transport Flotte	24
Sportschulen	6
SS Polizei	13
Staffs of the Inspectorates (colours)	49
Stalingrad	56
Steirische Heimatbund	22
Streifendienst	15,75,82
Sturmbootpioniere	8, 43
Suchteln bei Krefeld	43
Sudetenland Motor Gruppe	34, 36.
Supreme Group Commands	33
Supreme National Authority for German Motor Sport	4, 45
Supreme Command, Munich Offices of	41
Supreme Command, Berlin Offices of	42
Svelit, Norway	44.
Technische Führerschule	43, 48
TODT, Dr. Ing. Fritz	51, 58.
TODT, Brigade	57,58,60 61, 67.
TODT, Organisation, High Command, Depts of	74 - 81
TODT, Standarte	51, 57
TODT, Transport Gruppe	Foreward 39,58,62, 68,69,71, 74 - 82
Toulon, Verbindungsstab	20
Traffic Control Service	13, 33
Traffic Department	42
Traffic Regiment	13
Traffic Signs	17
Transport Flotte Speer	24
Transport Standarte "W"	25
Transport Staffel Moorweide	25
TRENDEL, GF. Ludwig	41
Truppenbetreung	77
Tübingen	43.
U-Gerät	76
Unterschlesien, Motor Gruppe	48
Verbindungsstab Toulon	20
Verkehrerziehungsdienst	13, 50
Verkehrsdienst	13, 33
Verkehrsstandarte Wien	13
Verkehrshilfdienst	17, 33
Verwaltungshauptamt und Kassenwalter	41
VOGEL, Oberleutnant	17
Volksdeutsche	12, 63
Vorsitzender des Gerichthofs	40.

	Paragraph
Waffen SS	Foreward
	13, 62,
	63, 69
Waffenmeisterei	76
Wartime driving prof. cert	7
Wasserpolizei	18
Wehrstaffeln	7
Wehrmannschaftstürme	22
Weimar Report	1
Welfare of Field Forces	77
West Wall	51
Wien	43
Wien, Motor Gruppe	8, 24
Wien, SA Brigade 90	36
Wiking, Abteilung	59
Winter Service	82
Winterdienst	82
Winterhilfe	31
Wirtschaftsamt	30
Wohlynia (Volksdeutsche)	12.
Znaim (Motor Standarte 296)	36
Zeesen, Holland	44.

An unrivalled insight into the Nazi State

Extremely rare historic wartime studies of Nazi Germany's Paramilitary Wings, Organisations, Documents and War Criminals, that were compiled by Supreme Headquarters Allied Expeditionary Forces (SHAEF) and other more clandestine agencies.

These reports illustrate what the Allies had learned about the Nazi state prior to the eventual disarming and demobilisation of German military forces, and also in assisting in the hunting of wanted war criminals and interrogation of those accused of collaborating with the German occupation authorities.

Full colour as in the original works as appropriate, unedited, containing some or all of the following: uniforms and insignia (colour uniform plates), a listing of personalities holding, details of organisation, ranks, orders of battle and wartime activities, and identity and other documents carried by German citizens and alien labour within the Third Reich, and of the citizens of Nazi-occupied Holland, Belgium and Luxembourg (colour plates).

IDENTITY DOCUMENTS IN GERMANY 1944

SB: 9781474536745

HB: 9781474536752

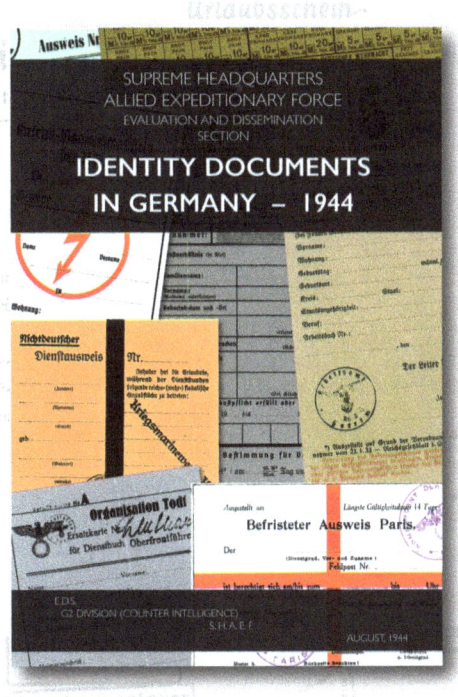

IDENTITY DOCUMENTS IN HOLLAND, BELGIUM AND LUXEMBOURG

SB: 9781474536882

HB: 9781474536899

THE NSKK OF THE NSDAP

Nationalsozialistisches Kraftfahrkorps – National Socialist Motor Corps

SB: 9781474536806

HB: 9781474536813

THE NSFK OF THE NSDAP

Nationalsozialistisches Fliegerkorps – National Socialist Flyers Corps

SB: 9781474536820

HB: 9781474536837

THE SA OF THE NAZI PARTY

Die Sturmabteilung Der NSDAP – Brownshirt or Storm Troop Formations

SB: 9781474536769

HB: 9781474536776

THE HITLER JUGEND
The Hitler Youth Organisation

SB: 9781474536844

HB: 9781474536851

HANDBOOK OF THE ORGANISATION TODT
The Civil And Military Engineering Organisation of Nazi Germany

SB: 9781474536783

HB: 9781474536790

THE REICHSARBEITSDIENST
Reichsarbeitsdienst (RAD) The German Labour Service

SB: 9781474536868

HB: 9781474536875

THE GERMAN POLICE

SB: 9781843425946

HB: 9781474536905

CROWCASS
Central Registry of War Criminals and Security Suspects. Wanted Lists
(The Nazi Hunter's Bible)

SB: 9781845742768

HB: 9781845742775

MILITARY HEADQUARTERS AND INSTALLATIONS IN GERMANY

SB: 9781843424420

www.ingramcontent.com/pod-product-compliance
Lightning Source LLC
Chambersburg PA
CBHW061547010526
44114CB00027B/2950